MY PURPLE PATCH

Living with ITP

MY PURPLE PATCH

Living with ITP

Anthony Paul Heard

The Author has asserted his right under the Copyright, Designs and Patents Act, 1988, to be identified as Author of this work.

All rights reserved. No part of this publication may be reproduced, stored in or introduced into a retriever system, or transmitted, in any form, or by any means (electronic, mechanical, photocopying, recording or otherwise) without the prior written permission of the publisher. Any person who does any unauthorised act in relation to this publication may be liable to criminal prosecution and civil claims for damages.

Copyright © 2019 Anthony Paul Heard
All Rights Reserved

ISBN Number - 9781728761800

Dedicated to my wife Amanda and in loving memory of my Dad - Alfie Heard 16/4/1922 - 7/7/1967.

Contents

Foreword
10

General Disclaimer
12

Useful Contacts
14

Always Tired and Bruising Like A Peach
16

I Cant Stand Up for Falling Down
27

But You Don't Look Sick
36

Waves of Doubt Keep Drowning Me
45

The Bitterest Pill Is Mine To Take
55

Itching after The Battle of Wounded Knee
63

Getting The Needle and Making my Hip Hop
71

Slow Slow, Drip Drip, Slow
77

Seeking Good Omens and Campaigning for Votes
86

Getting Social With Media and Speaking In The House
93

Going for Gold at London 2012 but Heading For A Fall
100

Walking On The Wild Side
107

The Moment You Know, You Know, You Know
114

What I Want Is Facts
121

Surviving The Alamo
129

Fatigue and ITP
136

Age Concern ?
147

If I Knew Back Then, What I Know Now
153

Starlings scoffed my Strawberries and Slugs savaged my Spinach
165

It Runs in the Blood
171

Banishing Ghosts of Christmas Past but Beware the Ides of March
182

Snakes and Ladders
191

Once I was Seven Years Old
197

Acknowledgements
205

About The Author
208

Appendix
211

.

Foreword

Staring at this completely blank page I ask myself why on earth I would want to torture myself by writing about my experiences with Immune Thromboctyopenia (ITP). After all, since I was diagnosed in July 2006, ITP has given me some of the most painful moments of my life. It has tested my mettle, my patience, my sanity and my physical well being. It has hardly been a walk in the park for my wife and family either.

Well the answer is actually in three parts.

Firstly I believe that writing about my ITP will be therapeutic. This sounds a bit like advice from Dr Frasier Crane the not so eminent psychologist in my favourite TV comedy *Frasier*. But I am convinced it will help. Revisiting some of the events of my ITP journey will remind me of exactly what did occur. Much of what was happening around me at the time, went by in a complete blur or in a scribbled diary entry.

Secondly, I hope that writing about my ITP may raise awareness of this mystery condition. Like most ITP sufferers I had never heard of it before I was diagnosed. I certainly had no idea what the symptoms were. Anything that I can do to raise awareness I am more than willing to try.

I have always believed that if you have a story to tell that you think will help other people, then you should tell it. The only way that we can learn from each other and advance our knowledge is to share our experiences, good and bad.

Finally, I hope that my story will help other ITP sufferers and their families better navigate the journey that we have been sent on. There is no standard map or guide book to get us through our individual ITP expedition. However, by telling my story I hope that it will be informative, occasionally amusing, often painful but certainly honest and definitely positive.

So if you are ready, let's go back to purple, my ITP story.

Welcome to My Purple Patch - My Life with ITP !

Anthony Paul Heard
July 2019

General Disclaimer

This book tells the story of my experience with the auto immune illness ITP (Immune Thrombocytopenia) . It should not be assumed that any of my experiences, symptoms, treatments or any of the responses or side effects I have encountered, will apply to other ITP sufferers. We are all different, we all show different symptoms, respond differently to the various treatments and encounter different side effects.

In no circumstances should anything I mention be taken as medical advice, and as ever, each case of ITP should be discussed with the individual's doctor, specialist or healthcare professional .

Always seek the advice of a healthcare professional if you have any concerns about your ITP or general health. The worst thing to do is ignore any symptoms you may have or try to second guess what may be wrong with you. In this dot.com age it is so tempting to look online for information and then self diagnose , BUT don't. Always see a doctor/ specialist/healthcare professional. Don't consult Alexa, Siri , do not google with your health !

In the following pages I will tell you my story, I will share with you my purple experiences but I can't diagnose your illness, give you platelets or cure your ITP. Hopefully I can give you some comfort, point out some of the pitfalls that I fell into and offer you a few interesting observations about ITP along the way. So here we go and what better place to start for absolute purple beginners than a few of the most useful ITP contacts, as listed on the next page.

Useful Contacts

The ITP Support Association
..www.itpsupport.org.uk

ITP Clinical Centres in the UK
http://www.ukitpforum.org/index.php/en/itp-clinical-centres

Contact A Family
https://contact.org.uk

Funny Blood
https://www.funnyblood.co.uk

The Platelet Disorder Support Association
..www.pdsa.org

ITP International Alliance
..www.globalitp.org

Patient UK
https://patient.info

Rare Disease UK
..www.raredisease.org.uk

CHAPTER ONE

Always Tired and Bruising Like A Peach

It still gives me a certain shiver of anxiety thinking back to that awful day in 2006 when my purple Odyssey began. Since then there has been plenty of drama, the odd tragic moment and even some comedy along the way. My very own epic ! What follows are my purple high and lowlights, a summary of my ITP so far. If you think it reads like a roller coaster, I can tell you that it was and in many ways still is. I should know, I've been there and I'm still standing !

The cunning nature of ITP meant that like many purple people I actually had the condition long before I was diagnosed with it. I now realise that I was suffering from Immune Thrombocytopenia for at least a year before it was ever confirmed. My lack of awareness of the condition and not knowing the symptoms, prevented me from taking action earlier to get myself checked. I did not realise that the symptoms I was experiencing were very dangerous, potentially fatal. Luckily I have survived to tell the tale. Hopefully my close shave might help others recognise the symptoms to look out for and the urgency needed to get checked out as soon as possible. It sounds dramatic but your life could actually depend on it. So here's an early tip, if in doubt get checked out !

My first hint of ITP dates back to early 2005. Sitting at my computer now, writing this all down, I had absolutely no idea then, that the strange random purple bruises and constant tiredness were a prelude to my purple adventure. The clues started manifesting themselves in Spring 2005. This was just over a year before I was finally diagnosed.

I started getting a few random, purple bruises on my legs and arms. These bruises were of variable size, some as small as a coin others as large as a jam jar lid. The one thing they had in common was that they appeared completely out of the blue. They

would not come as the result of a knock, bump, impact or blow. I thought they were simply accidental, albeit a bit strange. They seemed to fade or heal themselves within a week. I convinced myself that nothing sinister was going on. I simply continued with normal family and work life. I was really fooling myself.

As the summer of 2005 wore on and fell into Autumn the bruising started to increase in frequency, size and darkness of purple. In addition I recall being very tired, almost overwhelmed with fatigue. I also experienced irritability, wild mood swings from gloomy negativity to crazy over optimism. Especially at night, I also got itchy skin, particularly my hands, arms, legs, and feet. I quickly grasped that my tiredness was not something that could be cured by a quick nap. I was regularly feeling very weak and completely drained. I remember that in October 2005 I had one serious episode that made me think that I was about to collapse.

Looking back now, these symptoms were obviously clear signs that something very unusual was going on with my system, but nobody wants to believe the worst do they ? I'd been given more clues about something quite serious going on with my health than Poirot got on the *Orient Express*. But when we are going about our daily lives, none of us has any idea that a few quite odd, random symptoms are anything like as nasty as ITP. Besides which, I was simply too busy to be ill.

The pattern of random bruising continued through the winter of 2005. Some bruises were appearing overnight like a gift from the ITP equivalent of the tooth fairy. I would wake up with a purple patch on my person, completely random and of varying size and shape. In a couple of cases I actually saw bruises developing before my own eyes, on my hands and lower arms especially. I can only compare it to watching ink spread out on a sheet of blotting paper. The bruising was of course, blood leaking from my capillaries as my platelet count was so low that my blood clotting capability was dangerously low. I know that now but then, I was dancing in the dark.

Even with all those symptoms, I was only prompted to visit my doctor because I was constantly feeling tired and really fatigued. I was convinced that I was generally under the weather and might just be run down. During the consultation with my family doctor on Friday, July 28th 2006 I explained my constant tiredness and mentioned almost as a throwaway line that I had also been getting mysterious bruises for about a year. I casually mentioned that the week before our meeting I had been kneeling on the grass in our back garden pulling out some weeds and when I got up my knee caps were completely purple and remained so for a couple of days. I didn't experience any pain, so surely there was nothing to worry about ?

I thought that my doctor would think I was mad and even suggest that I might be inventing an illness. I had no idea that the tiredness and my purple rain of bruises could be linked in any way. I explained to her that I had been bruising like an overripe peach and constantly feeling tired for some while. My doctor looked a bit worried but surely I could not be causing her any concern, because after all, I had never been ill before in my life ? The only hospital encounters that I'd ever had were football related injuries, where a few stitches were required on a couple of occasions. I had enjoyed 46 years of trouble free health. Why would a few bruises and a bit of tiredness change anything? I had entered the surgery anticipating that my doctor would think that I was a hypochondriac but it soon became clear that she thought something serious may be going on with my health.

My doctor hinted that there was a chance that I was seriously ill. She did not say anything too alarming but examined the various purple patches on my arms, legs and torso then demanded that I have a blood test there and then. She was not prepared to say what might be wrong and would not comment further until the blood test results were processed. But I could tell from her demeanour that she thought I might have something seriously wrong with me.

She took my blood samples then I was sent home and advised that she would contact me by the end of the day with the results. I was told to stay at home and rest until we had news from the tests. On no account should I attempt to do anything strenuous I. All very mysterious, I thought, but I was not going to question a doctor's advice. To be honest, I was simply non-plussed by the whole thing.

So off I went on my merry, muddled way, slightly puzzled, and a little bit concerned. However, I still did not really think that it might be anything other than perhaps a virus just making me feel a bit run down. How wrong I was and on reflection, how dangerous it was for me to have driven myself home from the doctor's surgery that day. I dread to think what would have happened if I had been involved in any kind of accident. If I had received any kind of blow, especially to my head, it could have been fatal because as I was to find out later that fateful day, my platelet count (whatever that was) had fallen to a paltry four.

At 6pm on that very strange Friday, I received a phone call from my doctor and she was adamant that I needed to get myself to my nearest hospital Accident and Emergency Department without delay. I was ordered to attend the Royal Berkshire Hospital as soon as possible. She explained that my blood test results showed a very, very low platelet count and that I would probably need immediate treatment. I would most certainly undergo further tests to determine exactly what the problem might be.

Having spoken to my doctor, I was instructed to make sure I did not drive myself to the hospital and to avoid any blow or bump especially to my head . Apparently with such a low platelet count my blood clotting capability was negligible. It was serious. I was advised to pack a bag with some overnight things like sleepwear, razor (a battery or electric one as I must NOT use a bladed razor with such a low platelet count in case I should cut myself) and a change of clothes. I even remember her saying..." Don't forget your toothbrush ". I didn't really understand what all this meant at the time but simply tried to concentrate on doing as I was told.

My doctor wanted to avoid alarming me too much but she was clear that with a platelet count of just 4 it was potentially very serious. So having ended the call and still in a gibbering state at the end of the conversation I proceeded to try to explain all this to my wife. From that point on my wife took control and literally threw some random items into a holdall for me and drove me the five miles to the hospital. I cannot pretend that I was anything other than worried, confused and anxious. Once in the car and on our way to the hospital I tried to explain the telephone conversation that I had just had with our doctor. Neither of us could really compute what had been said or the full implications of it.

My anxiety increased when we arrived at the Royal Berkshire Hospital at 6.30pm because although there were many patients already in the waiting area to be assessed, I was taken straight through to a bed as soon as I reported to the Reception desk. My doctor had already contacted the hospital to let them know that I was on the way and that my case was very urgent. This is something that I only found out when I went back to see my doctor a couple of months afterwards.

At the time it got me thinking that if I was allowed to jump the queue, I must be very seriously ill. Jumping any queue in the UK is just not done, unless it is absolutely necessary, so as I was allowed to do so, I was clearly a serious case. I must have got some pretty ugly stares but I was way beyond capable of caring.

The nurses were very comforting and did as much as possible to calm my fears and anxieties. They emphasised that if the earlier platelet reading of 4 were correct it could be something that needed immediate treatment. They suggested that the earlier low count was very possibly incorrect. There was every chance that if they now did a few more blood tests the count would show a higher score. They advised me that our platelet count changes all the time anyway and it is rarely the same on 2 readings. The earlier platelet count of 4 could well be an anomaly.

More blood was then taken from both my arms and also from the back of both my hands. The samples were sent for analysis, primarily to check that the original test earlier in the day had been correct. We would soon see if my count really was as pathetic as 4. The samples would also be checked to see if there were any underlying issues causing the potentially low score if it really was that low. The nurses confirmed that only a blood test can confirm platelet count.

One of the many things I did not know then was that ITP is a condition diagnosed by process of exclusion. So ITP diagnosis is arrived at once it is concluded that all other possible diseases and problems have been ruled out. It is a case of all potential causes for a low platelet count being eliminated. Once they have been discounted, a diagnosis of ITP is the only option left.

The various blood samples were analysed over what seemed like an eternity. During this time I was examined by the doctors to make sure that I had no bleeding or that my general health was not subject to change. The usual vital indicators were taken and recorded every half hour. I had blood pressure, heart rate and temperature routinely measured albeit I had absolutely no idea exactly why at the time. There was just so much going on, it was almost impossible to absorb everything. In a strange way it meant that I didn't get much time to dwell on what might or might not be wrong with me.

It took about an hour for the duty doctor to confirm that my original blood test that day was absolutely correct. The sample that they took from me when I arrived in the hospital also showed a platelet count at that same meagre level of just 4. The doctor confirmed that this was very, very rare. That said, he was wonderfully reassuring and somehow confident that things would be fine. He checked that I had not had, nor ever had any bleeding and that my only symptoms had been tiredness and bruising. He mentioned the letters ITP but said that he could not say much more until the analysis of my blood samples had been fully completed.

By 11pm we were beginning to think that we would end up having to stay in the hospital overnight. But at last the doctor delivered the diagnosis of the cause of my almost non-existent platelet count. It is ITP he said and I could tell that he was relieved to say that. I had absolutely no idea what else they could possibly have been looking for. What else might have caused my platelets to disappear faster than something in a Houdini trick ? It is only now that I realise how much worse the diagnosis could have been, albeit ITP was obviously bad enough.

The doctor apologised that it had taken such a long time to get a diagnosis. He explained that as ITP is so rare, the hospital don't have a specialist on site at weekends and they had been discussing my case with him by phone. This business of being rare was to become a recurring theme and it remains so to this day. It is another reason why I have taken the time and trouble to tell my story. If ITP is not known then it is incumbent upon those of us who have been suffering from it to tell others about it. As President Barack Obama once said.... " Change will not come if we wait for some other person or some other time. We are the one's we've been waiting for. We are the change that we seek ".

In the end I did not need to use anything in my overnight bag that Friday as I was allowed to go home, packed off with some drugs called Prednisolone, Omeprazole and

Alendronic Acid. All three were to become very familiar to me over the next few years. For now, I was relieved that I could go home, safe in the knowledge that my condition was something called ITP, which was apparently controllable.

It had been a long, long night and I just couldn't wait to get home to sleep. I was to report back to a specialist at the hospital the following Monday to see how my platelet count responded to the drugs I was to take over the weekend. The specialist would explain ITP fully I and my many questions would be answered then. Oh if only it had been that simple ! The very fact that I was to meet my specialist at the Royal Berkshire Hospital Cancer Centre didn't help ease my mind over the weekend. The very mention of the word cancer, I have to say frightened me and I know that it really worried my wife too.

The problem is that when in the heat of the moment our logical, sensible side gets hijacked. Looking back on things now, it is obvious that if there had been anything really serious with my health, I would never have been allowed to go home that Friday night. But in the thick of the action then, the mind can only focus on the worst.

Tired and anxious but at least now with a diagnosis of what was wrong with me, not much else was said or explained on that Friday night. My wife and I eventually got home at around midnight. I was being allowed home because I had not experienced any symptoms apart from bruising and tiredness. If I had shown other ITP symptoms like bleeding from the nose, gums, or in my urine or stools they would have kept me in hospital for a few days as a precaution.

My wife and I were completely exhausted, confused, apprehensive and still in a daze. But just being able to go home was such a comforting feeling and it is something that none of us appreciate as much as we should until we have an experience as disturbing as a purple Friday night in AnE.

My first weekend as an ITP patient went by in a complete blur. Not surprisingly the confusion, worry and tension of being diagnosed took its' toll on me and my wife and family. I had started taking the tablets prescribed to me on the Friday night, but apart from feeling very tired, no other visible changes had taken place by the Monday.

I did notice a difference after about a week of taking the drugs with the impact of the 100 mg per day of Prednisolone being very good. I felt noticeably more energised. I was naive enough at that early stage, to think that all the negative side effects of the drug would not apply to me. I remember telling myself not to read the leaflet enclosed in the drug packaging. I was convinced that if I knew too much about the side effects I would talk myself into suffering from all of them. Ridiculous reasoning but when faced with new, intimidating situations it is amazing what we can talk ourselves into or out of believing.

Obviously, over the first few days as an official purple patient, I had no idea at all whether the Prednisolone was doing what it was supposed to do. Having had the medication explained to me at the hospital I understood it was meant to suppress my immune system so that it would stop destroying the Platelets that I was producing. So in theory my Platelet count should increase to acceptable, even normal levels.

Those first few days as a bona fide ITP sufferer got me asking a thousand questions and the main things that went through my mind that wobbly weekend were....

How did I get to be an ITP sufferer ? What had caused my immune system to malfunction? Was it my age, stress from work, diet ? Was it something that I could have inherited or caught ? Could it ever just go away ? How long would I need to take Prednisolone for ? How quickly would we know whether or not it was going to work ? What happens if it does not work ? What other treatment options are available ? Will I be able to carry on working ? What about flying, is it safe ? What should I eat or drink and what should I avoid ?

So many questions going around in my head and I was more than ready to put them to the specialist I went to see at the Royal Berkshire Hospital on Monday July 31st 2006 at 2pm. Everything would surely be explained to me at that appointment, albeit the most important aspect of that meeting was to be the blood test I would have beforehand. That test would show if I had responded to the Prednisolone that I had been taking since Friday. It was only 3 days but ever the optimist, I was convinced that my platelet numbers would have increased.

On arrival for my appointment, I realised that I was now officially an actual "case ". There was now something more permanent about my situation vis a vis the Royal Berkshire Hospital and my new status as an ITP patient. What had always been an arms length connection with the National Health Service had now become much more formal. The National Health Service and I would now be "in a relationship", not just passing strangers. I had an official patient number, I was in it for the long haul. My new file would attract paper at an alarming rate from now on.

The specialist made us feel completely at ease as soon as he met us. As always in Britain our meeting started with tea (what is it with us Brits & a very common hot beverage ?) . So a good, solid opening. Milk and one sugar. But even so my mind was bursting with all the things I wanted to ask. My stomach was like a tumble drier swirling with butterflies from fear, worry, concern, apprehension and tension.

My specialist explained that ITP is actually a disorder in which the sufferers' immune system destroys Platelets in our blood. ITP is an autoimmune disorder and causes a shortage of Platelets and in so doing hampers our blood clotting ability. This was all very well but I had no idea what Platelets really were, why they were important, what they actually do and why it mattered that I only had a handful of them. I just couldn't really compute what I was being told.

Nevertheless, he confirmed that Platelets are one of the key components which allow our blood to clot in the event of a cut or blow. So a shortage of Platelets means that we are at risk because if we suffer a blow or cut, we may not be able to form a clot properly to stop any bleeding. This shortage of Platelets was why I had been experiencing bruising over the last 12 months. They were totally random and would appear without any blow or knock because with my Platelet count so low, my blood was literally leaking from my capillaries. Think of it like a leak from a burst water pipe. Without plugging up the hole, the leak won't stop !

The specialist went on to tell us that ITP could arise in anyone at any time. It could not be caught from anyone else or passed on. It was not inherited and did not arise from stress, diet, age or type of work. At least there was no evidence to suggest it. ITP could develop in people of any age or ethnic group and we often cannot pinpoint any specific reason why it occurs in one person and not another. It can sometimes be a response to a cold, flu, virus, infection, or a reaction to a medication or vaccination but in many cases the cause is unknown. There was no cure for ITP but it could be controlled.

He admitted that ITP was pretty rare, with only about 4000 /5000 people suffering from it at any one time in the United Kingdom. He would probably only see a dozen or so new cases each year and ITP was officially defined as a rare disease. Suddenly I had not just become an ITP patient but a rare disease patient to boot ! For someone who had been ordinary for 46 years, I had randomly become extremely rare, but probably not in a good way.

By this time my blood test results were back from the sample I had given earlier that afternoon. My Platelet count had responded well to the 3 days of Prednislolone that I had taken and I now registered a count of 63. So already a staggering 59 higher than when diagnosed. My specialist was more relaxed after he had announced this good news. He said it gave him every reason to believe that my count would go back to the normal range of between 150 and 400 pretty quickly.

This good news was certainly very welcome BUT I still had so many questions and worries about what was happening to me and what I needed to do next. I was concerned about how long I might have to remain on Prednisolone? , how quickly could I start taking less of it ?, what side effects would I get ?, how quickly would the side effects start to kick in ?, what was the medication actually doing ?, would I need to be monitored regularly and if so how often ?, how would I manage to fit all this in with my work and the University degree I had just started ? So many things ran through my mind.

He explained that "safe " Platelet levels were anything over 50 for purposes of carrying out any surgery on a patient or having a tooth removed for example. A Platelet count of 30 would be deemed "safe" as far as not being dangerous or needing intervention (in most cases) . But each case needed to be considered individually, as we are all different, all have different medical history and show different symptoms. He confirmed that in general he looked to treat the symptoms not the platelet count.

For now I could take the Prednisolone at a lower dosage of 75 milligrams per day reducing from the 100mg I had started out on. In a week we would meet again, take another blood test and see what my Platelet count registered. I also needed to continue taking 20 mg of Omeprazole daily to mitigate the potential side effect of the Prednisolone of indigestion/heart burn. Looking further ahead, ideally my Platelet count would continue to rise and then we could reduce the Prednisolone dosage gradually by say 5 to 10 milligrams or so each week.

Apparently I could get on with my normal life, work and studies as usual. The only thing was to avoid getting any blows or cuts especially to the head. Also I needed to watch out for any other bleeding like from the gums, nose, urine or stools and any more of the random bruises that I was already well aware of. Although my Platelet count had already risen it was vital to look out for any of the symptoms just in case my count suddenly relapsed.

Before we finally departed, my specialist confirmed that I could eat or drink anything I liked albeit I needed to avoid aspirin, ibuprofen or quinine as they lower the Platelet count. So I should always avoid any products which contained quinine like tonic water, bitter lemon and some other drinks. Not forgetting that aspirin is an ingredient in many cold and hangover remedies. I was further advised I could find out a lot more about ITP in a leaflet he gave me from something called The ITP Support Association.This was to be the most useful piece of paper that I would pick up on my ITP journey.

My wife and I went home, kind of reassured, kind of apprehensive and kind of concerned. But the most obvious thing that we had already learned about ITP was that it was impossible to get a straight answer about anything. It was difficult to say anything that applied to every ITP patient. The only definite thing about ITP, appeared to be that nothing was definite ! We knew that the game was very much afoot and that we would be in for quite a bit of mettle testing in the future.

This journey was going to be unpredictable, uneven and more troublesome than either of us could have imagined. Turbulence was to become a frequent feature of our lives. Things would always come to depend on my platelet count, we would lurch from the best of times to the worst of times at the whim of a number. Just for the moment we did at least have the consolation that my Platelet count was 63, "safe" and almost half way to being "normal". But NOTHING would be NORMAL again from that day onwards. Although we would find a way to cope with it, we were destined to have quite a rocky ride with my new, rare foe. There would always be a purple elephant in the room, wherever I went from now on.

Chapter Two

I Cant Stand Up for Falling Down

Having responded quickly and positively to my Prednisolone dosage with an increase in my platelet count on July 31st, I was quite optimistic when I reported again to the hospital on Monday August 7th 2006. But that positivity soon evaporated as my platelet count had fallen to 37. My specialist was not concerned as he said that it takes a while for the platelet count to stabilise. He proved to be right because a week later on August 14th my count had risen to 51. This was good news as I had been on a reduced dosage of 60 milligrams of the steroid for 2 weeks. As a result my specialist confirmed that I could reduce my dosage to 50 milligrams and report back in another week. This all seemed quite positive and I went away in an optimistic frame of mind. I had no reason to think that I would very soon be hitting my own personal low.

But ITP sufferers will know that just when you start to think too positively, the ground tends to start moving under your feet. The old ITP carpet gets pulled and you flail about like a daddy long legs chasing its` own shadow across the ceiling. Well that is exactly what happened to me next. No, I did not chase my own shadow across the ceiling, but I did climb the walls and fall down the stairs of my own house. It was the most painful place that I have ever been and it was the place from which I HAD to start my fight back.

My sudden and unexplained descent into the darkest chasm of my life started on the evening of Monday August 14th. Without warning at around 6pm I started to feel very nauseous and dizzy. I was going from very hot sweats to shivering chills in the space of a few minutes. I spent all that night being sick, literally unable to keep a glass of water down. I knew that I urgently needed fluids because I had been vomiting so much. I would be in danger of de-hydrating but even a sip of water made me sick. I spent the night sleeping a little, sweating profusely and having to rush to the bathroom to be violently sick every time I awoke.

I had no idea what had caused this to happen. I could only assume that it was a tummy bug or virus which I had picked up. This was probably acquired easier than normal because I had been on steroids for 2 weeks and it makes us more vulnerable to viruses, colds, flus, infections and general un-wellness. Other than that it could have been a reaction to the steroids, who knows ? I do know that the next morning Tuesday August 15th I was so weak that I could barely stand up. My throat was so sore and dry from the strain that almost constant vomiting had put it under. I could not speak beyond a frail whisper. I sounded like a cross between Lee Marvin and Tom Waits. My voice was like a gate on rusty hinges. But amazingly I still had not yet reached my low point. Could it really get any worse ?

On that Tuesday I eventually got some water to stay down and managed to eat some plain yoghurt with a little honey. I could not face or eat anything solid but at least my system slowly recovered with some much needed re-hydration and light nourishment . I managed to eat a small bowl of chicken soup for supper and gradually began to feel less nauseous. It took me a couple more days before I could eat properly again but I felt that I was probably over the worst by the Thursday evening.

It says in my diary that on the Friday August 18th my wife and I went to the Theatre Royal Windsor to see the Noel Coward play *Private Lives*, so we must have gone because it says so. I have no recollection of it albeit I know the plot well having seen it before in the West End in 2001. We had booked tickets for the performance long before my ITP diagnosis and somehow, I got to the theatre and survived the show.

That theatre trip made my wife and I fully aware that our lives would never be the same again. From now on we had a third party in our marriage and our unwelcome intruder was ITP. No longer could we plan to do things without considering that horrible, intrusive third party. We would have to be more flexible and pragmatic. We would need to change our entire approach to life to accommodate my ITP. I cannot pretend that it was easy. In fact it was about to plunge me even further into the depths of despair.

Over the weekend of August 19th and 20th I was able to eat and drink normally without any problems and the nausea had completely gone just in time for my visit to the hospital for another blood test on the Monday August 21st. The result was desperately disappointing but looking back hardly surprising. My platelet count had fallen back to 17, albeit the nurses advised me that it was inevitable. They believed that I had been suffering from a nasty tummy virus and this would have reduced my platelet count.

When our immune system is faced with a virus, bug, infection or even a cold it puts maximum effort into fighting off that unwanted invader. In the meantime, because it is making a big push to expel the virus, it has less energy to produce platelets, so the net result is that our platelet count can fall. Here was another new piece of information that I had no idea of beforehand. I was certainly living and learning, albeit painfully.

My specialist advised me to keep taking the steroid at 50 milligrams per day for the next week when we would have yet another review. Since I had been diagnosed on July 28th I had already visited the hospital 4 times which literally doubled the amount of visits that I had made to any hospital in the previous 46 years. Some people on reaching middle age, do something a bit eccentric like get themselves a sports car, learn to play the clarinet or take up hang gliding but it seemed like my mid life crisis would be purple.

Ever the optimist I really did think that I might start getting better but little did I know that worse was to come the next day Tuesday August 22nd. What I remember about the episode now, is feeling so utterly helpless, so distraught, so childlike, so pathetic. Without sounding too dramatic, I felt out of control. I literally struggled to coordinate what I was doing and was unable to really focus properly. I know now that this situation was caused by the Prednisolone as my system was adjusting to being on a pretty high dosage. What took me to my pit of despair was actually something quite ridiculous but nevertheless it really did happen to me on that Tuesday morning.

I was, and still am lucky enough to work from home most of the time. On that bizarre Tuesday morning I was setting up my work schedule at 8:30 am and I wanted to treat myself to a cup of tea to kick start the morning. So i set about going downstairs to our kitchen to make a much needed brew. I do not remember using any of the stairs in my house to get to the ground floor that day. I literally fell down the entire staircase. I really flew. I had no control of my limbs and more worryingly I had no awareness of space or surroundings. I'd reached the bottom and I couldn't even stand up for falling down again. I was a complete wreck.

I was not feeling any physical pain from my sudden flight but I felt completely helpless, a bit like a tortoise turned over on its' back. How on Earth had I become so incapable, so haphazard, utterly useless ? I simply slumped at the bottom of the stairs in a collapsed heap and cried. These were tears of frustration as much as anything but they were the realisation of what a horrible state I had become. How had it come to this ? I just had no idea how I would ever get myself back on my two feet let alone back to health.

Undoubtedly what happened that day, was my body reacting to a tsunami of bad news/ill health. Almost certainly the side effects of the steroid were a major part of that. What I did not know then was that there were other, far greater forces at work but I will expand upon that in the final chapter of this book. It's complicated !

My unscheduled flight, without the assistance of a safety net was frightening. As I was in the house alone, I am just grateful that I did not suffer any actual physical damage from it. Thank goodness that I didn't hit my head. That Tuesday morning tumble, was the event that finally broke my spirit. For the first time in my adult life I no longer had control of my destiny. I had this completely random, purple interference invading my body. It was like a fifth columnist waiting to ambush me when I was least expecting it.

So I had reached the very bottom of my own stairs and arrived at my own personal darkest place. I resolved to myself, sitting on my own hallway floor that right there and then was my chance to fight back. I was having a very interesting conversation with myself at this stage. From this point on I would get back some measure of control. How I would do this I had not really worked out but I definitely would. With the help of my wife, family and friends I would start to accept my ITP but not let it dominate our lives. ITP would clearly, always be a part of me but it would not define me.

I had always been seen by everyone I had known or worked with as a very strong, reliable, resourceful character. I had been in some very senior positions and always been regarded as successful by those I had worked with. I am sure they would not have recognised the ghost of that same person who slumped on his own floor. I told myself that this fallen person was about to be history and the real me would bounce back. It's what I had always done in any adversity in my life. I was a fighter, more often than not a winner at most things I ever did. I would definitely beat ITP.

All these were fine words and intentions but the hours ahead let alone months and years that followed were not going to be quite such plain sailing. My brave words on that Tuesday morning, were admirable but actions were what counted. But at least I had now recognised that I had a real problem. ITP would never really go away, even if I went into remission it could come back at any time. I simply had to get myself up, dust myself down and move on. I was not sure what moving on actually meant but I knew that I had to do something to save my sanity, my physical well being and the health of my wife and family too.

I had been completely out of control and now I needed to draw up an action plan to get me on the road to recovery, after all without a proper plan you cannot achieve anything. Moving forward would turn out to be easier said than done and I am still working on it daily. But the fact that I am even writing this story must mean that I haven't done too badly.

Dragging myself up from the floor of my own hallway that day was the first move that I took towards complete acceptance of my illness. It was the biggest step of my life, even though I have had some wobbly steps and pretty painful times since. I have always looked upon it as a turning point. It seems dramatic to describe it as the beginning of the rest of my life but that is the truth of it. I suppose you could say that although it would never be the end in itself, it was definitely an end of the beginning of sorts.

The next thing I did was compose a list of things that I wanted to do in my life. I realised that in order to move forward I would have to plan ahead yet include and embrace my ITP. It was going to be a part of me whether I liked it or not. Concentrating on the things that I had always wanted to do would help to divert my attention away from my purple interloper and the side effects of the steroid treatment.

So my first scruffy list of goals were .....

Read more - Complete at least one book per week from now. Reading more, means writing better !

Complete my BA degree within the next 3 years.

Complete a Certificate in Humanities with the Open University within the next year.

Continue studies with the Open University after completing BA degree.

Help other ITP sufferers. Start spreading awareness.

Join the ITP Support Association.

Write a book about my ITP experience.

Visit museums, galleries, go to the theatre, concerts more often.

Start growing our own vegetables and fruit in our back garden.

Relax more, enjoy the moment. Focus on the now.

Looking back on them now all these things may seem very trivial. But I needed to re-state to myself the things that I wanted to do. I needed a reminder that I could actually still think about anything apart from ITP. It was almost as if my real self , had been temporarily taken over by my purple diagnosis.I needed to re-assert myself and quick. I had to acknowledge my illness and eventually fully accept it but not submit to it.

This was a good start but all of this did not detract from the awful side effects that started to kick in from the Prednisolone. In addition to waking up every morning at 2am and not being able to get back to sleep, I was snoozing at 4pm every day to compensate. On top of that I was beginning to see my face change shape, and the known characteristic of "moon face" started to develop as it does with many steroid users. I was feeling hungry all the time, completely ravenous and I was eating my food much too quickly. This invariably resulted in bouts of indigestion. Inevitably I was also starting to put on weight and feel generally uncomfortable , bloated and irritable.

I didn't understand that my response to the steroid was pretty much to be expected and was very similar to the impact Prednisolone has on many ITP sufferers. As pointed out by Greta Burroughs in her ITP book *Heartaches and Miracles*, she records her similar, wretched, initial reaction to taking the steroid....

" I had more get up and go than before I got sick. I was so wired and HUNGRY all the time. Several people had told me how Prednisolone increased appetite, but good Lord, I wanted to eat, eat, and eat some more ". Page 27.

In the same way as Greta, the steroid made me feel either, very optimistic and relaxed, or completely the opposite with quite angry, aggressive episodes. My moods were swinging more than Basie and Sinatra at The Sands. It was absolutely hell for my wife who could not really predict what I was going to be like from one hour to the next.

I was frequently irritable, tetchy, and at times clumsy, careless and out of sorts. I had episodes when I felt like Mr steroid Hyde would overtake me and turn my calm, pre ITP Jekyll into a nightmare for everyone around me. At the very darkest times it seemed like I was engulfed in the sort of miasma that I recall swaddling the London of my early childhood. Dickens referred to such fogs as The London Particular when the air was chewy with thick yellow smoke. My purple mist was never quite that dramatic but I often found it difficult to see clearly or think straight.

After a bit more time, I also encountered many of the other well known Prednisolone side effects and the worst for me were, cramp especially in my feet, aching muscles, particularly my thighs and calves, aching knee and elbow joints, headaches, hot sweats, flushing, a rash on my chest and spots/pimples on my face. Could all this really be happening to me ?

With all these physical and emotional changes starting to kick in I wondered if it was really worth continuing with the steroid, I began to think that the drugs don't work, they just make it worse and by the end of August 2006 I needed some good news. Thankfully on the 29th I got the lift I craved. My platelet count had increased to 59 from the 17 it had been on August 21st and I could now reduce my steroid dosage to 40 milligrams per day. It somehow convinced me that things would only get better from now on, albeit I soon came to realise that with ITP you can only ever really talk about the now. You really cannot get too far ahead of yourself.

With some good news, I felt that I could start to move forward as we ended August 2006. One of my key goals was to complete my BA degree with the Open University in the next 3 years and before that achieve a Certificate in Humanities within the next year. So I signed up to study a course entitled *From Enlightenment to Romanticism 1780-1830*. I was on my way. This was a hugely symbolic moment for me. It was proof that I really did mean what I had said when I had dragged my sorry self up from our hallway floor.

The ITP would just have to get used to the fact that I was going to do the things that I wanted to do. If my ITP was going to be a part of that then so be it. All that said, I was really struggling with waking up every morning at 2am and then not being able to get back to sleep. The Open University course gave me a welcome way to spend those sleep deprived hours. Instead of just passing away the wee small hours alone, I suddenly had such luminaries as Rousseau, Davey, Byron, Mozart, Sir John Soane, Delacroix, Owen, Goethe, Napoleon and Wallace to keep me company.

I found that studying also diverted my attention from constantly thinking about my ITP . My mind stopped focusing on what might happen, what my next platelet count might be, and many other questions at the back of my mind. Studying got me to think about other things, it forced me to push ITP into the background. It also gave me a bit of my sanity back and my wife & family were greatly relieved to see me in a more relaxed and positive frame of mind.

Like most ITP sufferers, I realised that it was a matter of going through a number of purple stages on my long journey. The first part of the voyage included shock, bewilderment, denial and anger. There were many steps along the route to complete acceptance. In the first few months after diagnosis, it was almost impossible to really understand what was happening to me. Everything just became a blur, I had so many questions, doubts, worries, and concerns. I couldn't really believe that I had been diagnosed with a rare condition which was to be my companion for the rest of my life. I not only couldn't believe it but denied it for a while. It had to be some sort of elaborate mistake, I had never been ill, I didn't do anything that would have invited illness. It simply couldn't be happening to me.

The denial transferred itself into anger after a few months. I just couldn't believe that someone as ordinary as me could have developed something as rare as ITP. I had never done anything that doctors constantly tell us to avoid. I had never been a smoker, never drank alcohol to excess, I had never taken any drugs, and I lived a healthy life in the main. I had always been a keen sportsman, and had continued playing football at quite a good level well into my 30's. My diagnosis just couldn't be right, it couldn't be true and I was getting more frustrated and angry by the whole thing.

Travelling towards acceptance of my illness was definitely made easier by resetting my goals and diverting my attention away from the rare intruder. Embarking on my studies with the Open University really helped me to stop worrying as much about my ITP. Put simply I had more important and rewarding things to focus on than a very rare condition which was apparently controllable anyway. Oh how naive I was !

I was driven on by the slow improvements in my platelet count and it gave me hope that as and when the count reached a near normal level (assuming it would), then I could be weaned off the drug. Hopefully I could even carry on thereafter without any further medication. Ever the optimist I just did not contemplate that there would be any reason why I wouldn't soon be off the medication and back to normal. Wishful thinking indeed !

CHAPTER THREE

But You Don't Look Sick

If I had a £ or $ for every person who had told me that I don't look sick during my ITP years, I would be a very wealthy man. I am sure that most people with ITP will have experienced this reaction from non purple folk. Most people simply cannot understand what ITP actually is and they find it difficult to comprehend that it often doesn't show any visible signs on the sufferer at all. I found it very frustrating trying to explain my ITP to other people. It is another one of the main reasons that I have worked hard to spread purple awareness by setting up and contributing to the social media platforms of the ITP Support Association, establishing my ITP blog and now writing this book.

Another very testing part of being diagnosed with ITP was coming to terms with the uncertainty. We are all creatures of habit. We thrive on the predictable and gorge on a diet of the familiar. But once in the land of ITP all of your previous thinking is turned on its' head. No longer is anything, (apart from the need for regular blood tests), certain, regular or definite. Trying to convey that to other people is so frustrating and a major challenge.

This very problem of trying to explain what it is like to be an ITP sufferer was another of the key topics covered by ITP sufferer Greta Burroughs in her excellent account of her own purple struggle *Heartaches and Miracles*. As Greta states…

"Life is hard having an obscure, chronic illness that no one understands. An ITPer can look or feel great or be depressed and fatigued. In either case, his/her body has a little war going on inside. It is very frustrating to hear comments like…"Well you don't look sick", or "At least you don't have cancer". Maybe not but we have an internal problem that has totally screwed up our lives. This is not meant as a slight against our caregivers but it is very difficult for friends and family to understand the dilemma we face unless they have been through it". Page 92.

What most people couldn't appreciate, and some still don't, is that it had taken ages for me as a sufferer to get my head around what ITP is . In fact, like most sufferers, I still have numerous unanswered questions myself even now. So then to attempt to explain it to someone else was always going to be a challenge. They were asking me all the questions that I was asking my doctors, nurses and specialists. It did get easier as time went by as I learned more about ITP myself. I suppose it was a bit like learning to ride a bike in that you start off very slowly, fall off a few times, dust yourself down and get back on again.

Even with the frustrations of trying to explain my illness to our parents and close friends, I had reasonable grounds for optimism in the Autumn of 2006. My platelet count rose to 77 on September 4th 2006, then 91 on September 11th and my steroid dosage was reduced to 30 milligrams per day. At this rate I figured that I would be back to a normal platelet count before Christmas and free of the dreaded steroid. Things had started to settle down a bit and my wife and I were determined to get on with life as normally as possible .

We went again to the Theatre Royal Windsor on September 12th to see a play called *The Hollow*. I have no recollection of it now but my wife reminds me that we had a very good supper at an Italian restaurant afterwards. I am certain I would have had plenty to eat and I would have eaten it more quickly than all the other diners. The steroid continued to play havoc with my eating habits and I became very self conscious about the unpleasant traits that I had developed.

I had become acutely aware of my ever increasing propensity to eat everything and anything at anytime. I was fully aware of it and embarrassed by my gluttonous appetite. I had morphed into a steroid fuelled Henry V111 impersonator in a Tudor banquet re-enactment. I started to think that I looked a bit like him too as my heft seemed to be doing its' best to grow into the role. I pictured myself as the portly King holding endless feasts at his Hampton Court Palace.

On the plus side, or should it be plus, plus side what with my expanding girth, my platelet count appeared to consistently be going in the right direction so my wife and I thought that we could tell more of our friends, colleagues and other relatives about my ITP. The reaction I got was entirely predictable and one that many other ITP sufferers will recognise. Most people responded by saying ...." But you don't look ill, you look absolutely fine". I did wonder how ill I was supposed to look or what "looking ill" really did look like. I mean, how do you judge ?

I know that most people were very well intentioned and of course meant no offence but in a delicate steroid state, none of this was what I wanted to hear. I learned to smile and mumble some sort of thank you for asking. But inside, although I was not quite steaming, I was gradually coming to a rolling boil. It was only after giving my family and friends a leaflet from the ITP Support Association explaining what ITP actually is that they realised the severity of the condition. I think having something in writing, an official brochure got the message across. What was rare, at least suddenly became real to them. I really was ill although I still didn't look it.

The problem is that many ITP patients, just like me, will have absolutely no outward signs at all of the illness. As I outlined in Chapter One, the only symptoms I ever had were the random, purple bruises and constantly feeling tired, irritable and fatigued. To all intents and purposes nobody would ever have suspected that I had any health issues at all, let alone a very serious yet rare autoimmune illness. This is how ITP is often experienced by many sufferers. It almost creeps up on you unnoticed, as if by stealth. Undoubtedly many people just like me may well have been suffering from ITP for quite some time before they are diagnosed.

My platelet count rose to 100 when I had my blood test on September 25th 2006. This was the first time my count had been back into 3 figures and my steroid dosage was reduced to 20 milligrams per day. I was still having the nasty side effects but at least I had the consolation of seeing the positive response in my platelet count. At the same time, work, family life and my Open University studies were keeping me busy so I considered that things were looking much more positive. I was still optimistic that I might be steroid free by Christmas. But with ITP of course, there is always a nagging doubt.

My platelet count and steroid dosage trend continued on the right trajectory when I had a blood test on October 9th 2006 and incredibly my count had reached 135.The drugs were reduced to 15 milligrams per day and our optimism surged. My count was still good on October 16th at 124 and again my steroid dosage was knocked down, this time to 12.5 milligrams per day.

With all this positive news my wife and I became much more confident about my treatment and the outlook generally. We had been assured from the outset by the specialists that my ITP could be controlled/managed and it seemed that they had been right. Unfortunately things would not continue to be that simple but having only been on the ITP ride for three months we had no idea of the numerous bumps that lay in the road ahead. We were still newbies.

But for the time being at least, our lives seemed to be settling down a bit, and we tried to carry on as best as we could with simply doing normal things. On October 20th we went to the Theatre Royal Windsor again and this time saw *Entertaining Angels*. It almost seemed that we had learned how to manage and cope with the steroid side effects now so it was possible to get out and about even more. We were determined to make the most of it . Looking back on that time I cannot but admire our determination but I am amazed at how innocent we were !

The good news continued on Monday October 30th when my platelet count had gone up again to 147. The steroid dosage was reduced again to 10 milligrams per day and my specialist felt confident enough to confirm that my platelet count was doing exactly what he had thought it would do. He encouraged us to get on with life and push ITP to the periphery of our thoughts. So taking this on board we asked him if it was possible for us to consider taking a holiday.

Our main concern was whether it was safe for me to fly with my ITP. He jokingly asked how I thought that I was going to fly without my ITP. He then reiterated that having ITP in itself was NOT something that should prevent the patient from flying. He would sanction my flight as long as my platelet count was over 50. That is the number that he wanted to work to bearing in mind that I had only been diagnosed for a fairly short time and we had only just started to see regular increases in my count. As my latest count was 147 he thought that it would be absolutely fine for us to book a holiday which we proceeded to do. All we now had to worry about was my count staying over 50 until our departure date on December 5th.

It is worth stating at this point that all ITP specialists and medical advisors are different in their opinions about what is a safe level of platelet count to work to. Each individual case is so different and we all have different responses to treatments, different pre - existing medical histories , different jobs, hobbies and numerous other things to build into the equation. It is always a matter of discussing your own case in full with your specialist. Only then can advice be specifically tailored to your individual situation. There is no one size fits all set of instructions with ITP and there never will be. What is appropriate for one person will not necessarily be right for another, albeit we can all benefit from sharing our individual experiences.

One really important point that my specialist made was that even though we were aiming to get my platelet count as high as possible and back within the normal range of 150 to 400 if we could, it was not JUST the platelet count that mattered. He was adamant that we must not get TOO hung up about the platelet count alone. With ITP, in his experience, it was important to take into account the symptoms that each patient shows or suffers. As previously stated, in my case I had never had any symptoms apart from bruising and tiredness. Other ITP sufferers might have had other symptoms like bleeding from the nose, gums, eyes, in their urine or stools even in extremely rare cases into the major organs or brain.

So in treating ITP he had numerous things to consider and the platelet count was just one aspect albeit a vital one of course. Another point he made was that it is difficult to predict at what level of platelet count each person experiences bruising or bleeding. As a general guide he would expect bruising or bleeding to appear once the count went below 20 but he emphasised that this was not always the case. Some ITP sufferers may find that they experience bleeding of varying severity when they had a platelet count well over 20. Any platelet count under 50 definitely needed to be monitored regularly and in his experience any count under 20 he would be looking to intervene with treatment. But even saying this he admitted once again that it would be each case on its' merits.

What I was beginning to pick up from all this new information and insight was that ITP was indeed a complete enigma. It seemed to me that there were very few certainties about this mystery condition. Just when I thought that I had got a solid answer about some aspect of ITP my specialist would add some sort of exception to the rule or caveat to his advice.The consolation for me at this point was that my platelet count was continuing to stay high, my steroid dosage was being reduced steadily and according to everyone who met me.... I still didn't look ill !

So after consulting with my specialist on October 30th 2006 after my blood test, and with my platelet count at 147 we booked a pre Christmas holiday to Boston. We were still a bit apprehensive about doing so but equally we were just determined to carry on with our lives. For the next month my platelet count would be under closer scrutiny than ever. Although it had been going up consistently, (albeit with the odd blip) since August, my specialist confirmed that he would only let me fly to the United States if the count remained over 50.

Well the crucial number continued to rise and on November 13th it reached 162 allowing the steroid dosage to reduce to 7.5 milligrams per day. Then on November 18th although my count fell a little to 140 my specialist saw no reason why we could not travel on

Tuesday December 5th. My steroid dosage was maintained at 7.5 milligrams per day but my specialist advised me that I must contact my travel insurance provider to confirm that they were able to provide cover for me as an ITP patient.

This was yet another point that I had not even considered so I telephoned our travel insurers and they confirmed that they did not need to impose any extra conditions or additional fees or premiums to insure me as an ITP sufferer. They confirmed this in writing and advised me to keep the letter with my travel insurance documents which they reminded me should be taken with me on my trip. In fact we took two copies of everything and my wife kept one copy and I kept the other just in case either of them went missing. It sounds like overkill but better safe than sorry.

All of this insurance related information is so important and it was yet another of the many things we had not really considered, mainly because we had never had any ill health before. Of course we have subsequently learned that not all insurers are as sympathetic or accommodating as our own. It is very important for anybody with ITP to talk to their insurers in detail about their health situation before travelling and make sure they are able to cover you. All insurance companies are different and have many different requirements, so check with them before you travel. It is also vital to advise the insurers of all medical conditions. The bottom line is that should you ever need to make a claim when you have not disclosed all relevant medical information beforehand, the insurers may decline to pay out.

So insurance policy checked and confirmed, bags packed, and in my case accompanied by plenty of platelets, off we went on our holiday/vacation.

Boston was a city that we had visited numerous times before but my ITP had never previously left the country. Flying out from Terminal 4 at London Heathrow on Tuesday December 5th at 10.54 am on British Airways flight to Logan International was quite straightforward for us. This time though, we now had an extra passenger with us. Excess baggage, you might say. How would my ITP passenger behave? Would I notice any difference? Would I be safe? Could I just forget about it?

Well we had six hours and twenty four minutes flying time to find out how things would turn out. A total of 3272 miles or 5266 kilometres flying at 36000 feet most of the way would be an interesting experience for us to say the least. Happily the flight was absolutely fine and it felt no different whatsoever from any pre ITP flight I had taken. It was just as tiring as any long haul flight would have been with the usual jet lag for a day or so afterwards.

Another difference on this trip was that I was carrying my stash of drugs. I made sure that I had ten days worth of my Prednisolone and Omeprazole dosage in my jacket pocket at all times. My wife also had exactly the same drugs haul too in case for any reason I lost mine. This did make for a certain degree of excitement when we were questioned by the Immigration official at Logan International Airport, on arrival. He was actually wonderfully charming and fully understood the situation. With our passports stamped we went to catch a taxi and after a twenty minute drive to our usual Boston hotel of choice The Marriott Prudential Centre, we reached our familiar destination.

We enjoyed a completely trouble free holiday and went about things with as great a degree of normality as we could. The only problem that my ITP gave us was my constant desire to eat, and to consume everything much quicker than is normal. That apart, we really had a great time and we visited all of our favourite places.... Newbury Street, the Prudential Centre, Quincy Market for great shopping, the North End for wonderful Italian food, Beacon Hill and the Common for the atmosphere of Old Boston, Cambridge for Harvard, North Station for Celtics and Bruins. We even managed to slot in a visit to the Boston Opera House to see a performance of *The Nutcracker* by Boston Ballet.

Best of all for me, a self confessed sports nut were visits to the TD Gardens to see the Boston Celtics play a home game against the New York Knicks and then later in the week to see the Boston Bruins play against the Montreal Canadians. The Celtics won but the Bruins lost. All in all we had a brilliant time and we managed to cram in a couple of visits to our favourite Boston eateries Abe and Louie`s on Boylston Street and Legal Seafoods in The Prudential Centre before heading back to the UK.

The flight back to Heathrow went without any hitches but two days after our return, it was yet another hospital appointment for me to get my platelet count checked. The great news was that on December 14th my count had increased slightly to 149 from the 140 figure of November 27th. A huge sigh of relief all round and I was permitted to reduce my steroid dosage to 5 milligrams per day to be checked again on December 28th. This meant that we could forget about hospital visits, blood tests and counts until after Christmas. It was a wonderful feeling but at the time we did not realise that with ITP, forgetting about these things can never be as easy as it sounds.

The reality is that whatever stage ITP is at, it can never be completely absent, it is like a shadow, a cross we ALWAYS bear. You can put your ITP jack back in its' box for a while but it doesn't guarantee that it'll stay there. But for now at least, Christmas 2006 we could enjoy things as much as normal and we managed to fit quite a lot into that festive season. We went to Borough Market in London on Saturday December 16th, had a great meal next to St Paul`s Cathedral then went to see the wonderful play *Coram Boy* at the Olivier Theatre on the South Bank.

Our Christmas went by without any health scares or incidents and we were thankful to spend it with our families in relative calm given the terrible anxieties we had all suffered since my ITP diagnosis in July. The last six months had been a real trial for us, and it was fair to say that 2006 was not going to be a year we would forget in a hurry. It was our annus horibilis albeit we didn't know then that there would be some pretty tricky times still to come.

On December 28th I returned to the hospital as appointed for another blood test and platelet check.The vital count had dropped a bit to 120 and so my steroid dosage was kept at 5 milligrams for a further 2 weeks when I would need to get yet another check. This was getting to be a pain, to say the least, but I had no choice but to return again to hospital on January 11th 2007 for another instalment. A new year beckoned, I still didn't look ill and I remained on the steroids but surely I would soon be allowed to drop them completely, wouldn't I ?

CHAPTER FOUR

Waves of Doubt Keep Drowning Me

So as Big Ben struck twelve to welcome in 2007 I had a comfortable platelet count of 120. As with the dawning of every New Year we always look upon it as a chance to wipe the slate clean, make some positive changes in our lives and purge the unwanted clutter. January 1st 2007 was no different and I reminded myself that whatever happened with my new unwanted purple side kick I was going to get on with my life. I'd crack this Immune thrombocytopenia surely !

All of that New Year positivity of course, quite often begins to dissolve as reality starts to bite. Nevertheless I was determined that my ITP was not going to prevent me and my wife & family from continuing to do the things we really wanted to do. We'd travelled to Boston in December 2006, had a wonderful holiday, enjoyed a great Christmas, and taken in numerous live theatre & music performances all since my diagnosis. I had got on with studying for my Open University Certificate in Humanities qualification, continued working and taken my ITP along with me, every step of the way.

The problem I was finding was that you could never really forget about the purple completely. It is always in the back of your mind, nagging away, a constant itch, a real attention seeker. I felt that I could never really escape from it. I was never more than a week away from my next hospital visit or blood test. Like most of us ITP folk, I was finding it all very trying, time consuming, not to say expensive what with parking fees at the hospital. The steroid certainly did not help. I was swinging between a wildly euphoric, optimistic maniac to the depths of despair within the same hour. Sleep was also a rarity at night because the steroid kept me awake albeit I filled the wee small hours with studying. I was putting on weight, eating like a horse, growing more chins and getting desperate to get off the wretched drug. I was seemingly trapped into a narcotic fuelled nocturnal existence.

My platelets continued to stay at good levels and on January 11th with a count of 149 I reduced my steroid dosage to 5mg every other day. My specialist confirmed that he would now taper me slowly off the steroid but it had to be done gradually. The steroid withdrawal can be tricky and it needs to be done at a sensible pace to help mitigate any nasty withdrawal symptoms. Whilst on the steroid our adrenal glands start to rely on it and in fact the steroid manufactures cortisol which is usually produced in our adrenal glands. So whilst we are taking the steroid the adrenal glands stop producing cortisol with the drug doing it for them. Getting off the steroid slowly allows the adrenal glands to adjust and start to produce the cortisol again. Other withdrawal symptoms can be, pain in the joints, arms, knees, ankles, sweating, hot flushes, low energy, listlessness and headaches. I got them all to varying degrees. Oh what a joy they were !

To be honest I paid scant attention to any of this at the time. I heard the words.... reduce your steroid dosage and then take you off them altogether, and that was all I wanted to hear. I was like the cat that had swallowed the canary. I was even blinkered enough to think I'd never have to take them or any other medication again. Six months on steroids, all done, ITP dragon slain, goodnight from him and goodnight from me. What can possibly go wrong ? Such wishful thinking !

Things continued to look good as on January 24th my platelet count was 139 so my dosage reduced to 2mg per day. By February 5th, more good news as my count was 147 and my dosage reduced to 1 mg per day. Things were going as well as we could have expected but the doubts were never far away. As ever with ITP you are only ever as healthy as your last blood test. It's like a purple Russian roulette. The illness is truly exhausting physically and even more so mentally. The purple keeps nagging away, it chirps in your ear repeatedly, reminding you that it will always be around.

My count fell a bit to 109 on February 19th but still I reduced my steroid intake to just 1mg every other day. Subsequently on March 5th even though my count had dropped a bit more to 87 the steroid was tapered further to 1mg twice a week. The grand exit from Prednisolone came on March 19th when my count was 101 and I happily stopped taking the drug completely. I was not required to attend the hospital for a further month. It was like winning the lottery, World Cup, 6 Nations, Olympic Gold, World Series, Stanley Cup all in one.

On reporting back to the hospital on April 16th my count was holding well at 91 and we remained hopeful that even without the steroid my platelets would stay steady and safe. This was confirmed on May 1st when the count remained at 91. But just as us seasoned ITP folk know, a fall is never far away. This was borne out on May 8th when the vital statistics revealed a platelet count of only 63. My specialist still remained confident that this was just a blip and indeed he was right.

As I had previously experienced, a key problem with taking steroids is that they suppress the immune system and in doing so it makes us more vulnerable to colds, flu, infections, viruses etc. I had picked up a cold which explained why my platelet count had fallen to 63 on May 8th. As mentioned previously, during a cold, virus, flu, infection the immune system is under pressure to fight it and in doing so it can impact on platelet production. Basically, fewer platelets may be produced hence reducing your count during the cold, flu, virus, illness.

So bearing this explanation in mind, I was slightly reassured by my specialist albeit those waves of doubt were, and never are held at bay completely. Sometimes, you feel a bit like King Canute trying to hold back the purple tide. However on June 4th with a platelet count of 98 and having been off the steroid since March 19th my specialist signed me off completely from his care. All I needed to do was keep an eye out for any symptoms and report back if I spotted any of them. So for now I would be hospital free, drug free and completely free to concentrate on revising for an academic exam.

I was to sit my Open University exam on June 12th and I was determined to pass as it would give me a Certificate in Humanities qualification. The studying I had been doing during my sleepless, steroid loaded nights was about to be tested. Would I be able to write about Davey, Wilberforce, Hulme, Rousseau, Goethe, Delacroix, Goya, Soane, Owen and others with sufficient clarity to earn the qualification I thought I deserved ? More importantly, would my platelet count hold up ? Would I suffer any steroid withdrawal symptoms on the day of the exam ? Would I get an awful headache or hot sweats ? Those waves of doubt kept rolling in you see but they were not going to completely drown me.

The exam was three hours long and it seemed more like twenty minutes. I remember writing so quickly, composing the essay answers in a structured manner but even though seemingly well planned, I was literally racing to finish on time. I was really focused, very energised and ploughed on through the various questions. I just felt so purposeful, almost stridently so, and slightly relieved to have made it to the exam with plenty of platelets on board. I had revised really thoroughly and I was eager to apply the information I had gathered. I was confident of my knowledge if still slightly wary of my platelet behaviour.

Even with a few purple doubts, the timing of the exam, was as right as it could have been. I felt like the cloud had finally lifted, albeit I didn't know then that the mist would descend again quite soon and return far too regularly thereafter. For the time being I was convinced that I had won the battle, but had I won the war ?

As we ITP sufferers know only too well, things are never quite that straight forward. Our enigmatic illness is a bit like a wasp at a picnic, the fly in your soup, the stone in your shoe. You can never quite be rid of it. And so, even having been dismissed from any further hospital visits for the time being, I still had a nagging doubt in the back of my mind that there was unfinished business with my purple foe. In the short run I was largely happy to dismiss the negatives. Having had to focus on my Open University exam it helped to direct my attention elsewhere. It was a wonderful distraction. I could ignore my uninvited guest for the moment.

In August I received good news that I had passed my Open University exam and got the award of a Certificate in Humanities qualification. I had somehow managed to sit the 3 hour exam and my result was a miraculous 81 per cent. Not bad for a steroid fuelled, narcoleptic, head aching, creaky joints suffering wreck. But I had really enjoyed studying and as I have stated it helped me tremendously.

I signed up to another Open University course straight away which would start in September. It would lead to me being awarded my BA degree if I could complete the course work and essays to the required standard then write a satisfactory dissertation. I could now get on with my studies, my normal family life and my job, knowing that I had no hospital visits ahead of me, no steroids or any medication to take. All I had to do was get a routine blood test in early September just to keep an eye on the platelet count. Plain sailing then, or at least it should have been !

My specialist said that I might get some withdrawal symptoms from the steroid but he was keen not to over emphasise them. He took the view that because we all react differently to these things it was best not to dwell on them for fear of having me focus on them too much. I got the point but it did not stop me suffering quite bad head aches and painful joints for a good while. Quite often I felt like a sailor on dry land, with sea legs still switched on when no longer needed.

I would often get very achy knees and wrists, especially when I got up in the morning. It was as if my joints had gone rusty overnight and it took quite a bit of effort to activate them fully each day. I'd go to bed at night feeling perfectly well and wake up in the morning like the Tin Man from *The Wizard of Oz.* This only really stopped completely, about 3 months after coming off the steroid but I was very heavily burdened during that time. I have since then learned quite a lot more about the side effects and withdrawal symptoms of steroids and as the old saying goes....if I knew then what I know now...I certainly would have been much more cautious about taking the steroid at all. Oh the benefit of hindsight !

It was a welcome treat being able to just get on with my normal life in Summer 2007 especially with my exam out of the way. I put my ITP behind me as far as possible. I got no bruising or other ITP symptoms following the withdrawal of the steroid. So from March 2007 until September 4th 2007 my ITP had to all intents and purposes gone away. It had disappeared as suddenly as it had arrived. Or had it ?

During this ITP intermission we made it a priority to make the most of our free time. So we squeezed in a visit to the *John Soane Museum* in Lincoln's Inn Fields Bloomsbury in March. Then lunch on the *Watercress Line* in April, a terrific performance of *Gaslight* at the Old Vic in June and a visit to Stanley Spencer's *Sandham Memorial Chapel* Newbury in July. But despite our generally positive outlook, it was never completely possible to forget my purple problem. What with the nasty withdrawal symptoms and nervousness about whether my platelet count would hold up, I was still apprehensive. It was almost as if I half expected a purple ambush at any moment. I didn't have long to wait.

Unfortunately, my blood test on September 4th came back with a platelet count of just 24. So it was back to see my specialist again on September 12th to discuss whether or not any treatment should be recommenced. I'd passed my Open University exam in June but failed my blood test in September and the conclusion was that we could not delay another round of steroid treatment any longer. My specialist was concerned that my count would fall even further and whilst I had not yet started bruising or showing any other symptoms, he was convinced that I would do so quite soon. As I was relatively new to ITP he did not wish to take any risks.

My count had dropped to 11 when I had a further blood test on September 12th, so we needed to get some steroids on board quickly to arrest the decline. One of the main advantages of steroids is that they do not take long to produce a response in the platelet count (if you are going to respond to them, you tend to do so within a matter of couple of weeks) . The other advantage about steroids is that they are cheap and can be prescribed, administered and taken very easily. Just a glass of water in the comfort of your own living room and that's all you need.

So here we go again, 100 mg per day of Prednisolone and 20mg per day of Omeprazole. My wife and I were disappointed but not as worried as when I was first diagnosed. I guess we had accepted the situation and had become resigned to it a bit. ITP was no longer a complete shock. The positive was that my platelet count had responded well and quickly to Prednisolone when I had it the first time. My specialist was certain that I would quickly get a positive response again. He turned out to be right but of course the horrible side effects were also quick in surfacing and they were just as persistent.

We just had to persevere, keep a watchful eye out for any bruising or bleeding, get back on the steroid and set off on another routine of weekly hospital visits. The blood tests were fine but it was the inconvenience that went with getting to the hospital, taking time away from work. It just grinds you down. I had got used to the crazy, almost manic, daily examination of my body for unexpected bruises, it became part of my daily routine . But as most ITP sufferers will know, the smallest bruise or mark that you see anywhere on your body sets off a completely disproportionate panic reaction. The ITP interloper, the wasp, the uninvited, unwanted pest is constantly buzzing around the mind if not always the body.

The Prednisolone did all the things that it was supposed to do and all the things we didn't want it to do too. My platelet count responded within a week of going back on the drug and it had risen from 11 to 64 by September 24th. Regrettably the unwanted side effects were just as keen and the sleepless nights, headaches, hot sweats, weight gain soon became evident again. At least this time around we had some idea of what might happen but to be honest it didn't make it any more bearable. The only consolation was that we didn't get any real surprises. Small mercies indeed.

By early November my platelet count had increased to 162. The steroid dosage was 15 mg per day having gradually reduced from 100mg since commencing on it again in September. My specialist confirmed that he hoped to remove me completely from the steroid by the end of the year, at the very worst. I was convinced that my steroids would be gone by the time Santa came calling. It was exactly the same conversation that we'd had a year ago and all I could think of was that I simply wanted to get on with the many things I had planned. I had a new Open University course to focus on for a start.

But a more pressing problem was looming on November 16th. A routine dental appointment would usually be completely straightforward, but I had never really given much thought to what ITP sufferers should do in respect of such matters. Would ITP make any difference to my dental treatment ? What should I tell my dentist about my illness, my medication, my current and future treatment ? Did he need to know ? Why did he need to know ? Could he treat me as a normal patient ? Could he treat me at all ?

For most people the merest hint of a dental appointment usually sets the collies wobbling. For some it's the buzzing of the drill, for others it's the smell of antiseptic or the taste of the mouth wash. Whatever turns us off, dental appointments are not much fun, unless of course unlimited nitrous oxide is dispensed. Ha ha ha ! I am fortunate that I have never had any concerns about getting dental treatment. I suppose I have tried to remember that the more you fear, the more fear finds you.

Luckily I have always had excellent treatment from my dentist Dr Bob An Ky To, at Blueberry Dental Surgery. I can't say that a visit to my dentist has ever held any concerns at all. It is more like catching up with one of the family with an inspection of my teeth thrown in for good measure. I guess I'm lucky in this respect. So my first visit to my dentist as an ITP patient shouldn't be any different, should it ?

Well, er, yes actually, it's very different. Just to make me slightly anxious I had heard from a number of ITP patients who had found it difficult to get a dentist to treat them at all. Others had indicated that they had great difficulty in finding a dentist who had any idea what ITP actually was. Surely things were not this bad ? It was 2007 not Victorian England where some people had wooden false teeth and some did DIY dentistry with pliers and string tied to door handles. Hard times indeed.

The importance of getting regular dental checks is so important whether or not you have ITP but once under the purple influence it becomes even more vital. The phrase prevention rather than cure always comes to the fore when thinking about dental checks but with ITP it is absolutely imperative. The last thing any of us with ITP needs is to have intrusive dental treatment, which is obviously going to be more difficult if we have a low platelet count. So by getting checked regularly and making sure we keep to good daily routines for oral hygiene, hopefully we can avoid treatment for things like fillings, gum disease and even extractions.

I knew that I had to tell my dentist that I had ITP. I needed to advise him what treatment I had received, what drugs I had been taking , what my latest platelet count was and what treatment regime I was gong to continue with. I knew all this because I had obtained a really useful leaflet from the ITP Support Association. It was very soberly entitled... Protocol for dentists treating patients with Thrombocytopenia. A protocol....sounded like something the UN would have drawn up. Why they couldn't just call it "Things a Dentist Needs to Know about ITP" ?. I don't know. But nevertheless it was extremely helpful and I gave a copy of it to my dentist at my appointment.

The daily Prednisolone sweats were over and done with by mid morning of my date with dentistry. So as my appointment was 2pm the only thing I had to worry about steroid wise, was dropping off to sleep mid - aaaaaaaaaaaaaagh ! As usual I'd been really suffering with no sleep at night and the steroids were keeping me awake all night, asleep during daylight. No surprise there, it's what steroids do.

I had learned to adjust my daily routines, to take account of the steroids making me generally hot and bothered mid morning. I would get hot flushes, sweating, general nausea and wonkiness around 10am and needed a quiet hour to see it off. So I adapted to doing most of my work, and any business meetings between 11am and 4pm. Then I would often take a nap from 4pm to 5pm and usually all would then proceed well or be passably bearable for the rest of the evening. I then went to bed at around 11pm only to wake again at around 2am. Overall, not an ideal routine but we had to make it work.

At the dental appointment, as ever, Dr Bob made things as easy as proverbial pie. He is just very good at what he does. He's so professional, well informed, up to date with all the latest technology and information (He didn't even pay me to say any of that !) I told him that since we'd last met I'd been diagnosed with something called ITP. Just like everyone else I'd told about my ITP, I thought he'd say something along the lines of ...... Well you don't look ill, I've never heard of it but I'm sure you'll be fine.

What he actually said was that although he didn't have any other patients with ITP, he'd heard of it. He would treat me in a similar way to a haemophiliac, although he realised that there were many, many differences. I sensed he was just warming up, so I gave him centre stage. He switched on his laptop and we looked up ITP. I'd given him my stodgily named Protocol for dentists leaflet, and he took a copy of it. He also looked up the ITP Support Association website there and then. I told you he was good !

He took notes as I told him my purple history to date. He recorded details of my drugs...Prednisolone, Omeprazole, Alendronic Acid, platelet count history, current treatment regime, name and contact details of my specialist and any other medical history of relevance. I didn't have any other medical history apart from ITP so within ten minutes, that was pretty much that. Drama over, we just needed to do the dental bit. Bring on the nitrous oxide ! Just open wide and Bob' s your uncle, or in this case your dentist.

It may seem obvious that our dentist needs to know our platelet count. If any treatment is needed, especially an extraction, a platelet count under 50 may preclude that treatment from being carried out. Advising our dentists of what medication we are currently taking and have taken for the last 12 months is also vital. Any drugs the dentist uses to anaesthetise us for example, may clash with any medications we have taken for our ITP or any other medical condition for that matter.

Another problem is that should we encounter any pain following any dental interventions the only painkillers we can take are Paracetamol. ITP sufferers must avoid Aspirin or Ibuprofen. Having purple in your life gives you so many things to think about.

Anyway, dental visit done and all teeth present, intact, cleaned and polished I was dismissed with my next check up booked for June 2008. I wondered what my platelets would be doing then and whether I would still be steroid free ?

The end of 2007 was fast approaching and we were boosted by very good platelet counts as the year waned. My counts were on November 26th at 162, December 4th at a stunning 200, December 19th at 176 and on New Year's Eve still very good at 158.

It was desperately disappointing that we had cancelled a planned pre Christmas break to Boston for mid December. But we needed some time for my platelets and general health to consolidate. After all, my wife and I had both been through more than enough turmoil since July 2006. Frankly we just wanted some peace, quiet, and rest.

My specialist had reduced my steroid dosage to 5mg per day by the end of 2007 and he was as keen as I was to withdraw me from it as soon as possible. On January 14th 2008 he delivered on his promise. With my platelet count at 158 I was again able to stop taking the chin doubling drug.

So that's all folks ! Done, dusted, steroid gone again, platelets at 158, dismissed from hospital visits. My expectations were so great, I thought I might bump into Philip Pirrip in the hospital car park. What could possibly go wrong this time ? Something told me that it wouldn't take long to find out.

CHAPTER FIVE

The Bitterest Pill Is Mine To Take

Having my specialist confirm that I could stop taking steroids from January 14th was the very best way to start 2008. My platelet count was 159 and this had been the second time that I had been on steroids since my ITP diagnosis in July 2006. I was just relieved to be weaned off the drug again. For now, yet again, I was optimistic that I could just get on with life without further interventions.

As all ITP sufferers who have taken Prednisolone know, the effects of the drug stay with you long after you have taken the last tablets. My weight had increased by about 6 kilos, my chins had doubled, my waist size inflated by 2 inches and my face was at full moon.

All ITP sufferers who have been prescribed Prednisolone will have some tales to tell about the side effects that they will undoubtedly have encountered. We all encounter some of them to one degree or another, albeit a few fortunate people only suffer mild problems. At worst, the side effects can be pretty severe. As ITP sufferer Greta Burroughs points out in her book *Heartaches and Miracles* on page 90….

"The side effects from some of the medications prescribed for ITP are life altering. For me, it was the cataracts caused by Prednisolone. The opinion that the treatments are sometimes worse than the disease is very prevalent among the folks that have been treated with steroids. The weight gain, joint pain, bloating, moon face, sleepless nights, gastrointestinal discomfort and mood swings are terrible ".

From Summer 2008 my immediate attentions turned again to my Open University studies, as my next course was about to start soon. I had plenty of pre course reading to do. I had my work cut out as I had to complete 6 essays and a dissertation to obtain my BA degree. So I really didn't have time for my attention seeking rare disease. ITP would simply have to go away....and for 2008 it did (mainly) ! But there is always a but isn't there?

I'd got news that the tutor who was to guide me through my Open University course was to be Dr Watson. I couldn't help but daydream that my tutor must surely have a close friend who smoked a pipe, played the violin, wore a deerstalker and lived in Baker Street. Perhaps, together they could solve the mystery of ITP ! Hopefully it would have an outcome more *Hound of the Baskervilles* than *Reichenbach Falls.* All joking aside, I couldn't wait to get started with my course and again it really did help to push ITP out of my thoughts, at least temporarily.

One key thing we'd already learned about ITP was that if you plan to do something important, then it seemed to be a cue for either a dramatic drop in platelet count or the day that the steroid side effects would be at their worst. We'd concluded that we needed to stay flexible about any arrangements we made for things like holidays, events, theatre performances or concerts. We accepted that although ITP would not stop us from doing things we wanted to do, it would make us more measured and better planned.

So it was not really a surprise that on May 10th 2008 we experienced a bit of a hiccup before an upcoming, pre booked holiday. We were due to fly out to Estoril, near Lisbon in Portugal for a 10 day vacation on June 2nd. Inevitably then on May 10th, ITP had to play its' hand.

As mentioned previously, I had become fully accustomed to the almost manic checking of my body every day for unexplained bruising. It seemed such a crazy thing to do but as all ITP sufferers will know it's just part of the routine. Anyway, on Saturday May 10th I spotted a suspicious bruise on the back of my hand. It was the all too familiar purple blemish and it was completely unexplained.

I had not had any blood tests since January 15th when my count was normal at 159. Since then I'd not had any symptoms or drugs at all. But this bruise on the back of my hand just got me in a panic. My wife and I kept trying to talk ourselves into explaining it as something I'd probably done by accident in the garden. Sadly, we both knew that neither of us would be able to rest or focus on anything else until I got checked out.

It is difficult to explain the blind panic that sets in when you discover a bruise or see anything that might be ITP related. It's just that you know that your own body is going through a civil war, with bits of it attacking other bits of it for no good reason. It's not Cavaliers versus Roundheads or Blues versus Greys. It's you versus er .... you. Like any war it is anything but civil and we find it difficult to fully comprehend. Sadly we face a constant battle when all we want is some stability and security.

But for us ITP folk the only way to be completely sure that we are safe is to get a blood test. Even though you might run the risk of being called a cyberchhondriac or one of the "worried well", it is imperative to get checked out if you are in doubt. Low platelet counts can seriously damage your health, in rare cases they can end it.

So here we were just weeks from going on holiday and faced with the prospect of our old foe making another unwanted appearance. The only thing we could do to settle the issue was go to the Royal Berkshire Hospital emergency unit and get a blood test. Now a visit to any hospital emergency department on any day is hardly at the top of anybody's wish list but such a visit on a Saturday is even less attractive. This is because our hospitals, sadly, are under even more pressure at weekends.

But what choice did we have ? The old ITP isn't something you can just ignore or trifle with. It's not just a small inconvenience. It's not like sitting behind a giraffe in a cinema, because hey, you can always change seats. No it's more threatening than that. Perhaps, at its' most acute it is like getting trapped in an elevator with a grizzly bear because without beating around the bush, ITP can be life threatening. It may be very, very rare that ITP can be fatal but bleeding into the brain or other major organs can occur and is extremely dangerous.

So off we set at 10am on that Saturday. The hospital emergency department was packed. Even when I explained that I was an ITP sufferer it did not get me seen any quicker. The triage nurse had a quick look at the bruise on my hand and asked if I'd had any other symptoms. When I confirmed that it was just the bruise she must have concluded that it was not serious enough to warrant bumping me up the queue. So like we do here in Britain, we just waited and waited, and queued and queued.

After an hour I had a blood test and was told to wait for the result. So we waited and waited, managed a cup of tea and a sandwich in the hospital cafe and just hoped the blood test would show a good platelet score. After another 2 hours the result came back showing a count of 64. During our wait we both concluded that our hospitals are not really hospitals any longer, but they are actually coffee shops with a sideline in healthcare thrown in. Harsh but it sometimes seems the case, albeit we are very grateful for what we have left of the National Health Service here in the UK.

Now the fun really started. The platelet count of 64 wasn't high enough for the emergency department just to discharge me without seeking the advice of an ITP specialist.

The problem was that they didn't have an ITP specialist to refer to on site and had to contact one by phone to seek guidance. ITP is so rare they just don't have a specialist on duty full time at weekends. It was exactly the same when I was originally diagnosed and remains the case to this day. So again we waited and waited, put some more money in the car park machine and went for more cups of tea.

After another 2 hours we eventually got confirmation that I was able to go home. The hospital had spoken to an ITP specialist and they felt that a platelet count of 64 was safe enough. They advised me just to keep a close eye on anything else that might be suspicious. So watch out for more bruising or blood in the gums, nose bleeds or blood in the urine or stools. If anything seemed unusual I should report back straight away. Other than that just get another blood test in 2 weeks time.

So there we were, 4pm and after 6 hours we were free to leave. We'd endured a rotten day. But at least I was safe. I'd been freed to go home from the hospital but I had begun to realise that as far as ITP is concerned.... you can check out any time you like but you can never leave ! A warm welcome to the Hotel California indeed !

I got another blood test 2 weeks later and my platelet count had jumped up to 95. So for the time being I was still in safe territory and still drug free. Better still, we were authorised by my specialist to go on our holiday to Portugal on June 2nd. We were just glad to have some much needed rest and relaxation to look forward to. We really needed a break, some sunshine, and time to unwind. So off we flew on June 2nd to Lisbon for our ten day break at the Hotel Palacio Estoril.

The only ITP baggage I had was our travel insurance policy with written confirmation from the insurance provider that they were happy to cover my ITP. In addition I took my steroid patient card, my Medical Emergency card, my ICH card and my SOS medical wrist band to wear at all times. But the good thing was I did not have any medication to take with me. I had been weaned off the Prednisolone in January so was still drug free, thank goodness. Whether this would last, and how long for, was anybody's guess but for the time being, we were just glad to be steroid free.

Our holiday was fantastic. Just having a break was a lovely feeling. The journey was straightforward, weather really sunny and warm. The Palacio Hotel, Estoril, Lisbon was wonderful. The food and wine excellent, platelets on good behaviour with no medication to worry about either. Apparently the hotel had played host to *James Bond* creator, Ian Fleming for large parts of WW2. Although I was feeling in good health during our 10 day spell at the Palacio, I still longed for some sort of secret agent to cure my dastardly illness. ITP had certainly shaken me and it had already stirred up some of my worst nightmares. At times, it had scared the living daylights out of me !

Returning to the UK, my full focus turned to completing my dissertation for my Open University course. I finished my project on British and French identity, before the deadline of August 31st and hoped it would be well rated by the examiners. Knowing that I'd done my best, even when my platelets had been trying to do their worst, gave me great satisfaction. I was proud to have completed that piece of work albeit it, I'm not entirely sure how I managed it. What with the steroid induced sleepless nights, increasing girth and heft, headaches, aching knee and ankle joints, general fatigue and ITP bruises (real, imagined and sometimes just dirt), I'm amazed I got it done.

The rest of 2008 went remarkably well and I remained steroid free and without any symptoms for the rest of the year. I got the fantastic news that my dissertation had been well rated by the Open University examiners and I was awarded my degree as a result in December. I was to attend the official cap and gown ceremony to confer me my degree in April 2009. I couldn't wait to attend the presentation, the culmination of 4 years hard, yet enjoyable work (2 of those years with ITP in tow). Everything seemed well set !!!

But, not quite, because, as ever our purple interloper had to have a say. Although I had not encountered any ITP symptoms, I had a strange feeling that the purple might make a reappearance. I had been feeling generally run down after Christmas & New Year 2008/9. So on February 25th, I reluctantly went to get a blood test at the hospital because I had been feeling such debilitating fatigue. My platelet count had fallen to 10. My specialist was surprised that I hadn't encountered any bruising or bleeding. I had not taken any medication for over a year and in that time, apart from my strange, random, false alarm bruise in May 2008, I had been fine. But now, yet again, it appeared that we had a problem.

My specialist insisted we try something a little different this time. We knew that my platelet count responded well and quite quickly to Prednisolone. So the suggestion was to start back on the steroid, just to get my count back to safe levels and then introduce a new weapon. The idea was for me to gradually reduce the steroid but at the same time take a drug called Azathioprine, which would, hopefully replace the steroid and, fingers crossed, keep my platelet count at good levels.

This new weapon, Azathioprine is a well established treatment. Like Prednisolone it would suppress my immune system, hence slowing down the destruction of my platelets, with the net result being an increase in my count. This sounded encouraging, it would get me off the steroid, and should raise the platelet count, with none of the debilitating side effects. But, as ever with ITP, my specialist added the usual warning that there are no guarantees it would work. But even so the prospect of no steroid side effects seduced me into immediate agreement.

So, stage one was to take the steroid at 60mg per day to get my count safe, then gradually reduce the dosage as the count climbed. Once the count was stable, we would introduce Azathioprine. The first part went very well and a normal count of 158 was achieved by April 6th.

So the steroid was gradually reduced from 60mg to 30mg per day and although I was suffering badly again with side effects, at least I was safe and well enough to go to my own Graduation Ceremony on April 18th. A cap and a gown, a shiny certificate and a few glasses of champagne were the least I deserved for all my studies. My wife and family deserved the freedom of the County of Berkshire for putting up with my purple and the wretched steroid induced mood swings. I don't know how they didn't murder me !

My counts stayed at good levels, so the steroid dosage was reduced to 20mg per day from April 24th. I was to start taking Azathioprine daily from then, along with the standard 20mg of Omeprazole. This all sounded like a solid plan and would gradually get me off the steroids for good. What could possibly go wrong this time ?

After the second day of taking Azathioprine I was incredibly sick. It was like a combination of being at sea in a force 10 gale, on an airplane in perpetual turbulence and drunk all at the same time. I broke out in hot sweats within 2 hours of taking the drug, with uncontrollable teeth chattering, shaking, very hot then very cold, nauseous, dizzy, room spinning and all the rest of the gang. All I could do was sit down and wait for it to pass. This took about an hour but I vowed that I would never take Azathioprine again. The bitterest pill really had been mine to take. If I'd taken it for a million years I couldn't have been any more ill ! What next then ?

My specialist agreed that I could not tolerate Azathioprine so we continued with a reducing steroid dosage, ditching our original plan. We also concluded that if I did have another relapse we would try a different treatment next time. We agreed to look at Rituximab. For now, ever the optimist, I didn't think it would happen. To be honest, I had become determined to just deal with the NOW, rather than look too far ahead. So with my count at 159 on June 29th 2009 the steroid was withdrawn again.

My very uncomfortable Azathioprine experience does not mean that Azathioprine will be wrong for other ITP sufferers. It could well be very successful for some and indeed has been. But like all things ITP, we are all different. We all respond in different ways to the various treatments, with varying degrees of success. For me, Azathioprine was, and is not an option but for others it might just be the saving grace.

What I did know by June 2009, was that with my platelet count at 159 and steroid free again, I needed another holiday. So Ciao Italia in September, platelets permitting.

CHAPTER SIX

Itching after The Battle of Wounded Knee

By June 2009 I was beginning to understand quite a bit more about my rare, enigmatic condition. I'd now been a member of the ITP club for almost 3 years. I'd already been on and then off Prednisolone 4 times and tried yet failed on Azathioprine with disturbing side effects. I realised that completely accepting that I actually had the illness was key to me moving on with my life. I'd conceded that whilst denial dulls the pain, it doesn't remove its' causes.

At the end of June 2009 my platelet count had reached a normal 159 and for the 4th time I was withdrawn from Prednisolone. My specialist and I agreed that if I should relapse again, I would try a drug called Rituximab next time, if there should be a next time. Although we were both pleased to see the steroid withdrawn I think we both knew that without it, my platelet count would probably fall again. But for the time being it was a question of getting on with life, hoping for the best but being prepared for the worst. We had the semblance of yet another plan.

As I have already mentioned , a very important thing that I had learned about my ITP was that as soon as you make a commitment to doing anything at all at a future date, then that is inevitably the time when things go wrong. That is the moment the platelet count falls, you notice a random bruise, you feel nauseous because of the side effects of the steroid, you get a thumping headache, tummy upset, or something completely random. It's inevitably related to ITP or the drugs being used to treat it. It's as if a purple ghost decides to haunt you when you put any firm commitments in your diary.

So almost inevitably on August 24th 2009 another completely mysterious, unexplained ailment arrived without invitation. It just had to turn up at that point, because we were due to go on holiday to the Adriatic coast in Italy on September 3rd. The old purple spoiler had to play a hand, or in this case a knee, in our vacation plans.

I woke up on that August morning with my right knee inexplicably swollen, very very painful, and totally seized up. The knee was literally 3 times its' normal size, I couldn't bend it at all, and I was unable to put any weight on it. I couldn't stand up or move unaided. This all happened without provocation, it just appeared overnight. All I could do was stay off it, take painkillers and put cold compresses on it to get the swelling down. But what had caused it, why had it appeared without warning, how long would it take to go, would it come back ?

After 2 days rest I was at least able to stand up and shuffle around. The swelling had gone down a bit but I still couldn't bend the knee very much. I did manage to hobble out of the house and clamber into the car for my wife to drive me to our doctor. I must have looked like an old man as I took an age to get from our car to the doctor's surgery. I was in a terrible amount of pain and I remember telling myself that this was surely as bad as it would get. It couldn't get any worse could it?

My doctor suggested that the wounded knee was probably due to a reaction to the heavy amounts of steroid I had taken in the last few years. Prednisolone is known to have a very bad long term impact on the joints, so unsurprisingly this could be the reason why I was suffering so badly. I suggested that it could be gout but as my knee showed no redness just swelling, my doctor thought it was unlikely. The truth is we were just not totally sure but it seemed very strange that it coincided with me taking the dreaded steroids.

I was told to rest for a week, take Paracetamol as required and ice the knee to get the swelling down. I was to report back to my doctor if things had not returned to normal within 7 days. So I was off the steroids but on the painkillers. I was almost completely immobile for another week. I was hobbling around the house with bags of frozen peas strapped to my right leg. I'm sure our neighbours must have seen me hopping around and wondered if I had lost my sanity but somehow the knee got better. The swelling went down, I got full mobility back and all was well again, at least for now. I'd won this battle of wounded knee but sadly there would be other injured legs in the future and even more painful episodes too.

But for now we got the good news that we could go away on holiday to Italy and we set off on September 3rd on our flight to Bologna. We travelled on from the red City by train to the Adriatic coast for some welcome rest, relaxation and sunshine. Now I am fully aware of the huge contradictions that make up the muddle that is Italy. I am partly Italian myself, so I should know. But the thing with Italy is that everyone has an opinion on absolutely everything. Not much ever gets done quickly, because nobody can agree on the best way to actually do it. That is part of the charm of the place and the people. So you can imagine the utter bemusement, confusion and agitation that my ITP caused when I tried to casually explain it to some Italian people we met on our holiday. Complete bewilderment !

We had a wonderful time in Italy, great food and wine, incredibly animated discussions about anything and everything. There was plenty of sunshine, the beautiful Adriatic coast, and no steroids, no swollen knees, stable platelets and for the moment at least, decent health. But as ever, the purple spectre is never slow in coming forward and sadly by November I was to be running on a low tank of platelets again.

On our return from Italy, things looked to be satisfactory with my platelet count at 103 on September 21st. But as is the case with many ITP sufferers the platelet count descends rapidly once it starts to fall. By November 3rd, my count was a pathetic 8. I'd been off the steroids since June 29th and it seemed that yet again we had reached another crossroads. Luckily I had not suffered any bruising or bleeding but obviously we needed to take some action before anything nasty did break out again.

My specialist put me back on the Prednisolone at 80mg per day, with a view to pushing up the platelet level to safe numbers. Then we would try Rituximab in the hope it would allow me to get a period of remission and steroid free to boot. So this was a clear and hopeful strategy. But nobody saw what was coming next !

As usual my platelet count responded well to being back on the steroid. I'd got to a count of 156 by November 16th, just 2 weeks after going back on the Prednisolone. So then on December 1st with my count at a very respectable 126, I didn't foresee anything that would derail my Christmas. How wrong could I be ? What was to come on December 7th was enough to derail the *Polar Express* , let alone me.

In accordance with the ancient unwritten law of ITP, yet again in December 2009 the familiar and uninvited interference from my unwelcome foe made an appearance. Just days before we were due to go to the Old Vic Theatre to see *Inherit the Wind*, and just a few weeks before Christmas, I got another painful reminder of just how wretched things could get with this rare illness. The purple puzzler was about to riddle again !

Over the weekend of December 5th and 6th , I had been very tired, hot, feverish and generally feeling like a cold or flu was coming. On the morning of Monday December 7th, I awoke to find that the entire lower half of my torso on the left hand side was aching, it was an angry red colour and very, very itchy. The area around my left hip, my back and my stomach looked like they had been burnt and the whole area was so painful. I could not bear to touch it and had great difficulty showering or even putting my clothes on.

As I was due to have a blood test that week to check my platelet count, I thought it best to go straight to the hospital to get my blood test done and my red, itchy patch checked out. I had no idea what it could possibly be and my wife and I thought it might be something as simple as an allergic reaction to something I had eaten, been bitten by, or even the washing powder we had used. If only it had been that simple !

On arrival at the hospital I had my blood test and the result came back quickly with a safe count of 116. But as I mentioned my unexplained rash, the itching and burning on my torso the nurses immediately rushed me into a separate room away from the other patients. The senior nurse asked to see the offending itchy area and straight away said ... It looks like shingles ! She then asked how long the rash had been on me, had I ever had chicken pox, when did I have chicken pox, had I been in contact recently with anyone who had chicken pox ?

My wife and I were utterly bemused. We had never given a thought to me having shingles. We didn't even realise it had any link to chicken pox and we had no idea why or how I might have suddenly contracted it. The nurse apologised that she had to put me in an isolation room. She explained that as the section of the hospital I visited for my blood test was the Royal Berkshire Cancer Centre and had some very vulnerable patients, her duty was to ensure they were protected from something as potentially dangerous as shingles.

The nurse however, reassured me as much as possible, explaining that in my case it looked like the shingles outbreak had only just happened. Because I had acted quickly I could be prescribed something to clear the virus. Taking quick action would mean that the virus could be cleared up fast before it might have the potential to become more serious. Could it really get any more serious ? I thought I had already had it serious enough but apparently there was more than a little extra potential danger available. How much more difficult could this get ?

I was sent to see my family doctor immediately. Apparently (and this is one of the crazy, irritating things I was discovering about our health service here in the UK), although the hospital were treating me for my ITP, and the development of shingles was clearly linked to my taking steroids, the hospital could not treat me for my shingles. This was the duty of my family doctor.

This seemed so ridiculous, but that's the way it worked apparently. It was just another example of the lack of joined up and integrated treatment that I personally had encountered. It is something that I know that Rare Disease UK have been looking at and campaigning to change. It really is so important, especially for folk like us who face so much uncertainty with our rare conditions. It's vital that a more coordinated, better integrated system is put in place. Maybe it's asking too much but surely it would save everyone time, money and stress. Just because it is difficult to change things, doesn't mean we should not at least try !

Anyway, on that frantic Monday morning we made a dash straight to my family doctor who was kind enough to see me without an appointment. He confirmed that I did indeed have shingles. It was in an early stage so that was good, if anything about it could be good. He explained that as I had been on and off, quite high doses of steroid since my ITP diagnosis in 2006, the action of the Prednisolone in suppressing my immune system had created the perfect environment for shingles to develop.

My family doctor went on to say that shingles is actually the reawakening of the Chicken Pox (Varicella-Zoster) virus . So if we have ever had chicken pox in our lives at any time, it can be reawakened if our immune systems are in any way run down or in the case of ITP, suppressed by drugs like Prednisolone, Azathioprine, Rituximab, Mycophenolate Mofetil . Having said all that, shingles does not reawaken in every one who is on these drugs , it is just more likely to happen if you have been on them long term.

This was yet another thing that my wife and I simply had no idea about. We looked at each other and in a knowing way we both shrugged our shoulders and sighed, as if to say ...Oh well, just another ITP related obstacle, bring on another round of another drug and we will try to get through it. This was beginning to feel a bit like the medical equivalent of the Blitz.

Like so much of my ITP story, the latest shingles episode just came out of the blue. It's the astonishing ignorance and naivety that really hit me, probably more than the shingles itself. I was just so astounded that I'd never heard of the possibility of contracting shingles, why hadn't I asked my specialist about all this when I was being bounced on and off the wretched steroids?

It was too late for questions now, so we just accepted that the next round of drugs would be something called Aciclovir, which I would take for 2 weeks at 800 mg, 5 times a day. I was to continue with my Prednisolone at 30mg per day, the Omeprazole at 20mg per day and Alendronic Acid at one tablet per week. For the first 46 years of my life I had taken no drugs at all apart from Paracetamol for a headache or toothache. Since July 2006, with my ITP on board, I had become a pharmacists' dream customer.

The feeling I could not shake off about my purple interloper was that every time I got some sort of painful episode from it, I couldn't quite believe that it would have anything else to throw at me. Surely it couldn't keep coming up with more trouble, more pain and more problems ? I'd had the awful dizziness, nausea, fevered reaction to Azathioprine. I'd fallen down the stairs in my own house without even noticing them, as the Prednisolone had taken hold. I'd had sleepless, steroid induced nights, swollen knees, weight gain, chin doubling, lunar face and now shingles. I was incapable of believing that I could get anything more painful. Surely it couldn't get any worse ?

The shingles episode was absolutely awful. I have never been in so much pain. Because the virus attacks the nerve endings and damages them, the area of the outbreak becomes so very sore. Our nerve endings are obviously very sensitive so any damage to them means that even the slightest touch to the area infected is tremendously painful, sore and itchy. If I found sleeping at night difficult because of the steroid, then the shingles doubled the stakes. It was as if my body had decided to play double or quits in the pain game and I had lost. Every night became a hard night's day. I just could not rest and certainly could not lay on or even touch the left hand side of my torso, abdomen or hip.

Agony was the word I could not get beyond, albeit the pain from my shingles did in a perverse way take my mind off worrying about my platelet count. Small mercies indeed. After a week of taking the Aciclovir medication the redness and anger in the shingles rash started to ease a bit. I was still going about my day to day life, including work, preparing for Christmas and trying to do things that would stop me thinking about the pain I was suffering.

My shingles attack continued to be very debilitating, although the anger and burning nature of the rash had gone down slightly, but it was still very painful. The entire Christmas and New Year period was very difficult, mainly because I could not sleep due to the discomfort of the shingled area on my body.

The rash and spots cleared up by the end of January 2010 but I was still suffering horrible pain from the remnants of the attack for ages after. In fact I still get some days when I feel a little itchiness and slight discomfort from the area of my hip, side and back. Shingles really was the Christmas gift that just kept giving.

This rotten episode delayed the plan that my specialist and I had agreed for treating my ITP. We had wanted to get my platelet levels consistently safe by using Prednisolone. Then we would gradually reduce the dosage as the count went up and introduce Rituximab in the hope that it would give me either full remission or at least an extended period, medication free. We simply had to end the steroid roller coaster. I couldn't tolerate any more of the Prednisolone and neither could my wife and family. I was going slightly loopy and driving them mad too !

So as the after effects of my shingles gradually receded during the Spring of 2010, and the platelet count kept at good levels, we reduced the steroid dosage slowly with the ultimate goal of having Rituximab treatment in early June. How lucky for me that it would coincide with my birthday ! We even cancelled our planned holiday to Vienna to make sure we had clear diaries to accommodate the next purple chapter.

Well, as usual with ITP things didn't go quite that smoothly. My platelet count started to bounce around and from a really good level of 203 in February it plummeted to just 49 by the end of May. By this time I was on just 5mg of the steroid and we increased my dosage to 15mg per day for 4 weeks meaning the the original plan for Rituximab in early June had to be put off until mid July. But my specialist felt that we just had to go for it, without further delay. So all we had to do now was have a simple procedure called a Bone Marrow Test (often referred to as a Biopsy or Aspiration) .

So the innocent sounding, yet wretched Bone Marrow Test was booked in for July 12th at 2pm. My platelet count was 63 and assuming everything was satisfactory from the test my first round of Rituximab would be given to me on Friday July 16th. What could possibly go wrong, surely nothing could be even more painful than all the trouble that I'd had with shingles since Christmas ? Well guess what, it could.

CHAPTER SEVEN

Getting The Needle and Making my Hip Hop

By June 2010 I had been on and off the Prednisolone rollercoaster 4 times and had endured a very dizzy Azathioprine experience. My ITP diagnosis in July 2006 now seemed an age ago. I had endured so much in 4 years with a lot of it, seemingly due to repeated, high dose steroid usage. But with my platelets still misbehaving every time the steroid was withdrawn, we had to try something different. It had become apparent that there would be no sudden appearance from John Wayne or even Bruce Wayne to save the day.

My specialist kept reassuring me that we would eventually find the right treatment for me. He remained completely positive that I would eventually get one of the treatments to give me sustained remission from my ITP. What surprised me more than anything though was that I now readily called my illness MY ITP. I really had come to own my illness, it definitely was a part of me. I suppose that you could say that I had fully accepted it. I don't really know when that acceptance actually struck me but it had. I don't recall a sudden happening or eureka moment but more a sort of gradual erosion. Almost a gentle submission I suppose.

In that Summer of 2010 it was clear I couldn't tolerate any more of the awful steroid side effects. Added to the wretchedness of the side effects, using steroids long term, clearly increased the risks of other health problems. Every time I looked in the mirror at myself, all I could see was a picture of billowing plumpness. Added to all this, I'd already encountered terrible pain from completely unprovoked swelling in my right knee during the Summer/Autumn of 2009. Then at Christmas and New Year 2009/10 I had contracted shingles. Add to this, the mood swings, headaches, face at full moon and chins multiplying, it all underlined how important it was for me to try another approach.

The new weapon was to be Rituximab and my treatment was to start on Friday July 16th 2010. But before that I was to have a bone marrow test on Monday July 12th at 2pm. My specialist advised me this was being done to check that my platelet production was not in any way abnormal. The test would also check red and white blood cells and confirm whether the bone marrow was functioning properly.

My wife and I had a few days off during the first week of July, simply to get a break from thinking about my ITP as much as anything else. We had got tickets to see one of my musical heroes Tony Bennett at the Royal Albert Hall on July 1st and no platelet shortage was going to stop us going. Needless to say he was amazing and even though the voice was not as strong as it once was, his timing, phrasing and stage craft were still top class. What a legend the man is. His life, really has been the Good Life ! I admire him so much as a singer, musician and artist but more importantly as a human being. He has always been at the front of the queue when it comes to standing up for what is right. The other obvious thing about him is that we share the same first name and we also both have Italian heritage. How could I not be a fan ?

But soon enough it was back to matters ITP. I was advised that the bone marrow test would take about half an hour but to be prepared to rest at the hospital for an hour or so after as I might feel a bit sore. I was told to be accompanied on the day as it would be inadvisable to drive myself home after the procedure. The test could be quite painful but usually only for a very short time (a matter of a few minutes). I would be given a local anaesthetic to numb the area where the bone marrow sample would be taken from. On the whole, it was a simple procedure, nothing to worry about and all over with in a flash. At leat, that was what my specialist told me.

A thick needle is used to take samples of bone marrow (the soft, jelly-like tissue found in the hollow centre of large bones). Bone marrow biopsies can be carried out for a number of different reasons, including to find out why you have a low or high number of red blood cells, white blood cells or platelets. A large number of different health conditions may be responsible for these types of blood abnormalities. Where a diagnosis has already been made, samples of bone marrow may be taken to check how well treatment is working – for example, in leukaemia or to fully confirm that the original diagnosis was correct.

Bone marrow biopsies are usually taken from the top of the pelvic bone, just below your waist (the hip area). You usually have a local anaesthetic to numb the area, and you may also be given a sedative to help you relax and cope with any discomfort or anxiety. I did not have a sedative but probably would elect to do so if I'd known then, what I know now.

The bone marrow biopsy then, is used to help determine the cause of a number of possible abnormalities, which can include: anemia, or a low red blood cell count, bone marrow diseases, such as myelofibrosis or myelodysplastic syndrome, blood cell conditions, such as leukopenia, thrombocytopenia, or polycythemia, cancers of the bone marrow or blood, such as leukemia or lymphomas, hemochromatosis, infection or fever of unknown origin.

Our bone marrow is the spongy tissue inside our bones. It's home to blood vessels and stem cells that help produce, red and white blood cells, platelets, fat, cartilage, bone. There are two types of marrow: red and yellow. Red marrow is mainly found in our flat bones such as our hip and vertebrae. As we age, more of our marrow becomes yellow due to an increase in fat cells.

I was pre warned about the very short, sharp pain that I might get from the bone marrow test. I was expecting a bit of discomfort but I was not ready for the excruciating, agony that I did get. The bone marrow sample was taken from my hip bone. Sometimes it can be taken from the chest bone but in most cases it is the hip . I was given a blood pressure, temperature and heart rate check before anything was done. Then I was asked to lay on the hospital bed and turn onto my left hand side. I was given an anaesthetic at the top of my right hip. This numbed the whole area and it took about 15 minutes for it to kick in. I was then ready to get the needle.

The said needle was inserted into my right hand side near my hip to take the sample. I could hardly feel anything as the needle went in through my skin and burrowed down. I was fairly well padded around my hip, thanks in the main to the steroid and the heft it had encouraged over the last 4 years. I only started to feel uncomfortable once the needle hit the bone. The real agony started when the needle was taken out again. This unleashed my inner Vesuvius. I can't think of anything else to describe how my system reacted. It was indeed like a volcanic eruption. My entire body flinched and recoiled as I could feel my system reacting to the violent procedure it was being exposed to.

I could feel an upward flood or surge from my feet to the top of my head as my body responded with an outpouring of heat. I sensed my temperature rise as it reacted to the pain. Fortunately this was all over within about 2 or 3 minutes, although it seemed like a fortnight. I have never had any pain like it, before or since. It made my shingles agony seem like a stroll in the park with an ice cream. The only consolation was that it was over very quickly, but the needle had definitely made my hip hop and my body pop.

For some strange reason, throughout the whole procedure I was singing in my head the fantastic Johnny Cash song... *Five Feet High and Rising*. It is crazy what our minds start to engage in when faced with pain, crisis, agony and being out of our comfort zone.

I kept asking myself... How high's the water mama ? during that bone marrow test and somehow it got me through. Johnny Cash has always been another of my musical heroes and since that bone marrow test he has taken an even more significant place in my personal hall of fame.

Once the procedure was completed the doctor confirmed the sample had been obtained as required. But I was advised to remain lying down on the bed for twenty minutes to allow my system to rest and recover. I then sat up on the bed for a further tweety minutes and had a very welcome cup of tea. I usually take one spoonful of sugar with a cup of tea, but on this occasion I could have taken one hundred and one to steady my nerves. I started to feel much better after about an hour and I couldn't really feel any more pain at that time. It is incredible how quickly our bodies can adapt, adjust and recover, thank goodness.

My wife had accompanied me to the hospital and I was just so happy to have someone with me. I was also relieved that she could be our driver as it would have been quite painful for me to have driven home that afternoon. The other wonderful thing about having her with me was that we talked about all the things we wanted to do once I got through the bone marrow biopsy and subsequent treatment. It took my mind off the pain and gave me something else to focus on.

One and a half hours after the procedure was completed I was allowed to go home. I was advised to take Paracetamol if I got any pain from what was after all a nasty, invasive test. A light dressing was stuck over the area of my hip where the needle went in. I was instructed to keep the area dry for 2 days. It made for very difficult showering and bathing but somehow I managed. Thankfully I did not get anything other than a bit of soreness and aching for the next few days. I left the dressing on for the rest of the week and it was removed when I went back to the hospital on July 16th for my first round of Rituximab treatment.

The wound from the bone marrow test healed completely within about 10 days and I got no further pain thereafter. All I have are the memories of one of the most wretched experiences of my life. It may not have taken long but that bone marrow biopsy was as painful a procedure as I have ever endured and I certainly wouldn't want to have another one any time soon.

I felt myself quite fortunate that I didn't get any further pain in the days after the bone marrow biopsy. I was made fully aware that bone marrow tests can give some people a lot of pain after it is done. It is certainly very important to be cautious for a few days after the test. It does take a while for our system to recover. Some people take longer to get over these things than others. My specialist had reiterated that I should definitely avoid strenuous activities for 3 days to avoid opening the wound . I should contact him immediately if I got any bleeding, increased pain, swelling, drainage or fever. Luckily I had no further such complications.

My bone marrow test result confirmed that there were no abnormalities in the production of my red or white cells or platelets. So I was now all clear to commence my Rituximab treatment on Friday July 16th at 9am. It was like getting the go ahead for take off from air traffic control. I'd definitely got my slot. I was a little apprehensive about it but I knew that I couldn't go on with any more debilitating Prednisolone episodes. The new approach might have risks but they were worth taking to give me a steroid free future. Somehow I knew that I was ready to give it a shot, I was willing to *Walk the Line* and step into that burning *Ring of Fire* !

CHAPTER EIGHT

Slow Slow, Drip Drip, Slow

My first infusion of Rituximab came on Friday July 16th 2010. I can't say that I wasn't apprehensive about it. I had done some research and it raised more than a few concerns. But I had to try a new treatment strategy. I couldn't possibly go on with Prednisolone after having it four times since July 2006. I couldn't tolerate Azathioprine so Rituximab was worth a try, even though, it clearly had some risks.

I was aware from my research that Rituximab (UK), or Rituxan (USA) is a Chimerical Monoclonal Antibody (a very specific antibody for a single target) designed to act against the protein CD20 found on the surface of immune system B cells. It destroys B Cells and is used to treat diseases/conditions characterised by excessive numbers of B cells, overactive or dysfunctional B Cells (including Lymphomas, Leuutyakemia, organ transplant rejection or auto immune diseases).

So Rituximab destroys malignant and normal B cells that have the CD20 protein attached to them, as it binds to the CD20 protein on the B cells. It is the protein CD20 which, once attached to the B Cells, is then responsible for Platelets being destroyed in the spleen. The actual purpose of the CD20 protein itself is unknown.

I understood that it was an antibody developed in mice and it has been used regularly "off label" in treating ITP. It had also been used to treat Rheumatoid Arthritis, Multiple Sclerosis, Evans Syndrome, Chronic Fatigue Syndrome, Systemic Lupus Erythematosis & in the management of kidney transplant recipients. So it was not specifically licensed to treat ITP but results from it had been good. My specialist was pretty confident it would give me at least 2 years remission, possibly more.

The prospect of being free from steroids was the key as far as I was concerned. I just wanted to get back to something of my old self. I missed being the optimistic, positive person I'd been before steroids changed things. I'd grown in many ways with steroids, not least my waist size, blood pressure and chins. But in truth, what had reduced with the steroid, was the quality of my life, and that of my wife and family. I'd fought hard and kept trying to put a brave face on things but undoubtedly Prednisolone was no longer the path for me to tread. I'd been there, done that and got the t-shirt four times, starting with medium and ending up with extra large !

So Friday July 16th 2010, zero hour 9am was my first round with Rituximab and I was as well prepared for it as I could be. I had been told by my specialist that the first dosage is given very, very slowly so I would be at the hospital all day. He suggested I take plenty of things with me to keep me occupied. He also advised me to wear comfortable, loose fitting clothing as I would literally be laying on a bed or sitting in a chair all day.

Another point he made was that I should be accompanied for my treatment because driving myself home after such a long day would be inadvisable. So my wife as ever, suffered my treatment as much I did as she endured the entire process with me. We made sure that we had plenty of books, a few newspapers & magazines plus a picnic basket packed with food and drink. We'd taken less on some holidays for goodness sake !

I knew that Rituximab is given by 4 intravenous doses with a week between each dose. It can take up to 3 months for the platelet count to respond to it but we are all different in our response times. Sadly some people will not see a positive platelet count response at all. The main negative is that it suppresses the immune system and for up to 6 months after having it, you will be more vulnerable to getting colds, flus, viruses, infections. Within a matter of ten days I was about to find that out for myself.

I had been allocated a bed at the day clinic of the hospital and after checking in, I was advised to get up on the bed albeit I could remain sitting up. It was suggested that it is best to be on the bed at least for the first couple of hours of the treatment. This was just as a precaution in case I had an adverse reaction to the drug. This seemed sensible but didn't really relax my nerves very much.

Then the nurses took my temperature, blood pressure and heart rate. These tests were repeated every half hour for the rest of the day. I was then given a heated pad to put on my left arm/hand to warm up my veins. An intravenous (IV) line was then put into my left hand and all I had to do then was take the pre-medication drugs (Pre - meds).

I was given a Paracetamol tablet and the other two pre - med drugs were Piriton (an antihistamine) and Cortisol (a steroid) . I was advised that it would be a further half hour until my bag of Rituximab would be hooked up to the IV line dangling awkwardly from my left arm. Apparently the Rituximab had to be delivered from the lab to the hospital and it would not arrive until 10am. The dosage I was to be given was 375mg/m2. at each of the 4 treatment sessions.

So for half an hour I tried to have as normal a conversation as I could with my wife but I couldn't stop feeling nervous and apprehensive about what was to come. I don't think any of us can feel anything but even just a bit anxious when we are in such alien situations. But I just kept thinking about the prospect of being steroid free once my treatment was completed. I was optimistic that it would work even though I knew my 4 rounds of treatment were going to be long and exhausting days.

Finally at 10am my Rituximab was plugged into my left hand/arm and for the next 7 hours we would be inseparable. For the first hour of the treatment I was confined to my bed as a precaution but after that I could, in theory take my valuable friend with me anywhere I wanted within the confines of the hospital ward. If I needed to go to the bathroom, get a cup of tea or coffee, have a glass of water, my expensive friend would come with me. I was stuck with it and it was stuck with me.

Everything started out fine, I literally couldn't feel anything happening at all. The IV line was a bit tricky to get used to and slightly awkward but other than that I felt reasonably comfortable, albeit a bit cumbersome.

The drug was being dripped into my arm very, very slowly and I tried to avoid looking at the bag full of costly fluid. It was dangling precariously from a flimsy looking drip holder that resembled a hat stand. I couldn't bear to look at it because the bag was emptying so agonisingly slowly. At the rate it was reducing I knew that I was going to have a very, very long day. It really was... Slow, slow, drip, drip, slow. Every glance I made at the clock on the wall showed that time itself was ticking and sticking in treacle.

The wonderful nurses explained that Rituximab is given at such a slow rate (especially the first infusion), because it can sometimes provoke an allergic reaction in the patient. They calmly explained that usually the reaction is quite minor but they always err on the side of caution. This is also why my temperature, blood pressure and heart rate were being monitored every half hour.

About an hour and a half into that first dosage I got a very sore throat and developed a rash in the centre of my chest with a little tightness in my breathing. This is a common reaction apparently. So the nurses stopped the treatment for an hour to make sure I did not get any further adverse response. I did not have any further problems but it meant my first dosage took that much longer to deliver.

It was indeed a long day, in fact the longest and most exhausting day I'd had in a while. Things were especially tricky when I had to take my valuable friend and its' hat stand to the bathroom with me. It must have looked like I was trying to do an impersonation of an inebriated Fred Astaire as I slowly shuffled around the ward. If I'd have known I might have worn my white tie and tails. I certainly didn't cut a dash as the hat stand had a will of its' own and the wheels on it seemed to go in the opposite direction to the one I was pointing them in. I was literally waltzing round and round with this crazy, dizzy contraption. Unfortunately it was more Charlie Chaplin than Fred Astaire. I was hardly the epitome of elegance. A dash, I did not cut !

A brilliant summary of my Rituximab experience is captured by Danny Baker in his terrific book *Going on the Turn*, the third volume of his memoirs. He writes a harrowing account of his treatment for head and neck cancer, covering his chemotherapy and radiotherapy sessions. Reading his description of the chemotherapy treatment brought all the memories of my own Rituximab infusions flooding back. I could readily identify with so much of what he said and I make no apology for quoting directly from pages 165 to 167 because so much of it was exactly what I had been thinking. Obviously where he mentions chemotherapy, substitute the word Rituximab but otherwise he reflects my feelings entirely. So this is what he said ....

"In fact, and I'll be completely honest with you here, until that morning I did't even know how chemotherapy was administered. If they had stuck me under a heat lamp or asked me to drink from a glowing flask, I would have gone along with it. I knew there was an element of intravenous business but was this merely preparation or one of the stages ? What nobody had forewarned me about was that chemotherapy is without question the most boring of all the treatments available to modern medicine. And when I say boring, I don't mean to be flip about either its' study, field or superhuman results. It is merely a balls-achingly dull experience. "

He continues.. " Here's how it went for me. A needle is slipped into a vein at the back of your hand, and - following dozens of checks that you are the intended recipient - this is then connected to a bulging bag of chemicals that really does have skull and crossbones on it. This slowly, extremely slowly empties its' contents one minuscule drop at a time into your system. You can neither feel any apparent benefit nor discomfort. You just sit there. A digital display counts down the hours you have till the bag is 100 per cent empty, which is a decision that gainsays all visual evidence. The chemo bag may shrivel so it looks like an old bit of bacon packaging that has been left for decades in the Gobi desert, but that clock will tell you there is in fact more than another hour to go before the shrill pips of it's alarm signal that not a drop of chemo remains ".

"Then, guess what ? The hospital staff take the desiccated bag from its' metal pole and replace it with one full of clear saline to wash both the system and your body through. This bag takes just as long to filter down. Then , guess what ? The whole tortuous tedious imprisoning process has to start all over again. Don't let anyone tell you that there is only twenty-four hours in a day. A day on the chemo drip is as long as any on that notoriously dawdling planet Mercury- and a wet Mercury bank holiday at that. No composer, no author, no director has yet created a work that can distract from the interminable hours spent being made well by this sluggardly miracle cure ".

I really couldn't have put it any better myself, and thank goodness that like me, Danny responded well to his treatment albeit in both our cases it was not exactly plain sailing.

My first expensive bag of Rituximab had finally dripped all of its' contents into my body after 7 hours. It was 5pm and the hat stand, empty bag and IV line were dismantled and taken away. I could actually move my left arm fully again and I could go to the bathroom without a dizzying waltz. I was detained at the hospital for another hour to rest and get used to being fully mobile again. My temperature, heart rate and blood pressure were also taken for the final time before I was dismissed. Everything seemed to be normal.

I didn't show any physical scars from that long day apart from a bruise on the back of my left hand where the IV line had been inserted. But I felt absolutely exhausted, mentally and physically. Apart from being a complete leap in the dark, the entire experience was just so tedious, slow and draining. Once it was all over I could have slept, standing up. I just wanted to get home, have a hot bath and sleep.

I felt slightly better the next day for having slept soundly for about 12 hours. But apart from tiredness I had no other noticeable side effects. The only thing that kept going round in my mind was that I still had another 3 days of the same treatment to come over the next 3 weeks. Oh what joy and plenty of opportunities for another few sessions of waltzing with my valuable friend and its' crazy hat stand. A few more inebriated Fred Astaire impersonations but hardly putting on the Ritz.

For the next week, I couldn't stop asking myself a whole host of questions.... Would my platelet count rise from the level of 63 it was before my first round of treatment ? As I was still on 10mg per day of Prednisolone, would I ever be able to get off the steroid? Would I get any side effects from the Rituximab? Would the second round of treatment be quicker than the 7 hours the first dosage had taken?

My Round 2 with Rituximab was scheduled for Friday July 23rd. Once again I checked in at the hospital at 9am and the routine was exactly the same as for my first tranche of the treatment. I was again allocated a bed for the day and I knew that the treatment could take anything up to 7 hours. The nurses reassured me that they expected my 2nd round of treatment and indeed my 3rd and 4th to take significantly less time than my 1st round.

My left hand/arm was once again to be the target for the IV line and before anything was connected up for my treatment to start, a blood test was taken for a platelet check. The result from the test would not be back until later that afternoon and it would be a useful indicator to see if my system had responded to the first round of treatment a week ago.

Just as with my first tranche of treatment, I had my premedication drugs about 30 to 45 minutes before my 2nd round started. This would be exactly the same on my 3rd and 4th rounds too. The premedication drugs were once again a Paracetamol tablet, an antihistamine called Piriton and a steroid Cortisol. So we were all set, ding - ding round 2.

My 2nd bag of skull and crossbones emblazoned Rituximab was hooked up to my IV line at 10am and I knew it was just a matter of sitting back, relaxing as best as I could and letting the drug slowly infuse into my system. I was again attached, for better or worse, to my hat stand via IV line . We would be inseparable for the day and again I would clumsily drag it around with me whenever I needed to visit the bathroom or just stretch my legs.

I did not get any reaction at all during my 2nd round of treatment, so it was much quicker than the first. I had emptied the very expensive bag of my drug in 5 and a half hours, which was 1 and a half hours quicker than my first round. This was all positive news and it made me feel a bit more optimistic to know that hopefully the 3rd and 4th rounds might be less arduous too.

The IV line was removed at 3:30pm and I was asked to wait for a further hour to rest and relax before I was allowed home. But before my dismissal there was the small matter of the blood test result from earlier in the day. Depressingly my platelet count had actually fallen slightly. I had registered a score of 60 which was down from 63 on July 16th, the day of my first round of treatment.

The nurses and my wife tried to cheer me up when I received the news. They realised that I was simply fed up with the whole, taxing process. They said all the right things and made me realise that even at a count of 60 , I was still in relatively good shape. Obviously we were hoping for better but patience was needed. This was always going to be a long game and we had been warned that Rituximab can take a while to have a positive impact on the platelet count.

A bit flat and quite frustrated by the whole purple thing, we trooped off home just hoping that next week when round 3 was due, my platelets might start showing themselves in a better light. I already knew that I was to remain on 10 mg per day of the steroid until after round 4 of the Rituximab, so whatever happened my Prednisolone sentence was not going to end just yet.

What I didn't know on that Friday night was that by the Monday morning of July 26th I would be struck down with a terrible cold, cough, sore throat, general aches, pains and all the rest of the wretchedness of a virus. I rang the hospital to let them know how this unwelcome development had sprung upon me over the weekend.They confirmed that it was something that is quite common following any Rituximab infusion.

Like Prednisolone, Azathioprine and Mycophenolate, Rituximab is an immune suppressing drug. The combination of me still being on the steroid and having 2 rounds of treatment had inevitably weakened my resistance to colds, flus, viral infections and so I would be confined to my bed for the next ten days. It meant that my 3rd infusion would have to be delayed. I needed to rest and allow my system to recuperate. So my scheduled visit to the hospital for Rituximab 3 on July 29th was postponed. I would eventually have the treatment on Friday August 6th.

At that 3rd round of treatment, everything went very smoothly. I had no adverse reaction at all and I was finished in 5 hours. The other incredible news was that my platelet count had increased to 112. This was literally dumb founding. I had thought that if an ITP sufferer gets a cold, flu, virus, infection the platelet count would go down. So here we were with my count having risen from 60 on July 23rd to 112 , even though I'd had ten awful days with a rotten cold, cough and splutter. This was when I knew we MIGHT be in business with Rituximab. Perhaps I wasn't living in a land of clouded cuckoo's after all.

I couldn't pretend to really know how my count had risen, I was actually expecting a slight fall. Despite all logic my count had bounced up. All I could conclude was that Rituximab had really started to do the job we'd hoped it would. I just realised that once again ITP was a complete enigma and I accepted that I just didn't understand all the science at all. Regardless of all that, to be honest I didn't really care, my count had gone up, positive news at last.

My 4th and final round of treatment was concluded on Friday August 13th (yes, I know, Friday the 13th). Even without avoiding black cats and ladders it went without a hitch and my stay at the hospital that day was over by 3pm. What made things even better was that my platelet count had remained good and was 102. I was authorised to reduce my Prednisolone dosage to 5mg per day and dismissed from visiting the hospital for a month. My specialist was confident that Rituximab had started to do its' work, but as I said at the time, "fine words don't butter any parsnips".

I felt like at last I might be making progress and I was hopeful that I could soon rid myself of the steroid and those awful side effects. For the first time since July 2006, perhaps I could actually just get back to living Prednisolone free again ! I had endured so much since my ITP diagnosis but I'd actually achieved quite a lot in spite of it. I'd obtained my BA degree with the Open University in 2008 but I honestly felt that I was probably only running at about 60per cent of my capabilities. So now if I could just have a good period without the steroid perhaps I could get back to firing on nearly all cylinders.

My next blood test and check up would be on Monday September 6th when we would get a better understanding of how I had responded to Rituximab. Until then it was very much a case of keeping optimistic that it would work. I had learned that it did not pay to get my hopes up too high, because quite frankly they had been let down quicker than a balloon with a puncture too many times already.

The thing that I kept remembering was that all of the many treatments for ITP are pretty serious drugs. None of them are risk free and all of them have quite nasty side effects. All of the medicines need to be considered thoroughly with a specialist before embarking on a course of treatment. The numerous options are all a bit of a leap in the dark and we can never be completely certain how we are going to respond or react. The various options offer hope but it's not like choosing your dessert from the pudding trolley. They all have potentially serious long term implications for your health and well being.

So a cautiously calm approach was my method of attack but I cannot say that I wasn't just a little bit apprehensive about how I would respond to Rituximab. Like anyone else, there is always a certain degree of trepidation. The only consolation was that I wouldn't have too long to find out. To be honest Monday September 6th couldn't come soon enough ! I was desperate to find out my fate.

CHAPTER NINE

Seeking Good Omens and Campaigning for Votes

The date is Monday September 6th 2010 it is 8.30 am and I am standing in a queue of six people at the reception desk of South Block Clinic at The Royal Berkshire Hospital Reading. I am waiting to check in for my 11am appointment with my specialist. I have become a regular at this clinic since I was diagnosed with ITP in July 2006 and I've slipped into a well rehearsed routine.

My cunning plan is to arrive at least an hour and a half before my appointment as this ensures that I get a space in the always, overcrowded hospital car park. This morning I get a good space and this must surely be a good omen. I proceed to check in at the clinic reception desk to make sure that I can get all the pre appointment formalities done promptly. The first thing is to advise the reception desk that I've arrived. This allows them to get my ever expanding file ready for my appointment.

The reception team recognise me now and comforting smiles pass between us as they wish me luck for my appointment today. I proceed to the holding area where the duty nurse is stationed to weigh all patients attending clinic. Again we recognise each other, and exchange greetings as I am taken to the unforgiving scales. The nurse notes down my current weight and adds it to my file notes which my specialist will see later. I vow to start cutting down my calorie intake and do more exercise just as I always do. She confirms that my file notes are growing much more rapidly than my girth.

Amazingly I have actually lost a couple of pounds since my last check up, so that is perhaps another good omen. Perhaps all other vital numbers might go in the right direction later. After dozens of visits I am amazed that I still insist on clinging to things like good omens. Even things like a small weight loss convince me that today my platelet reading will be safe. Because you see, it is a positive sign and obviously that HAS to be a good omen.

Following my weigh in, the duty nurse asks me as usual when I had my last blood test. She knows that my answer is always the same but automatically asks the question each time. I always have a blood test straight after my weigh in, so I advise her that I am just going to the blood test clinic now. It is part of my routine and superstition suggests that if I change my routine it might bring bad luck and a low platelet count. I just cannot take that risk.

I have a blood test form which I was given at my last check up in June. In fact I have a valuable currency in my possession in blood test clinic world. You see, my form has a priceless green spot attached to the top right hand corner. Without the magical green spot, indicating that I am an urgent case needing priority, I would probably face a wait of at least an hour. I wave my form at the senior nurse and I am called straight in for my test. I sense the piercing stares of the twenty pairs of eyes of those sitting in the queue which I have now jumped. The magic of a green spot has sent them all green with envy and I feel quite guilty but at the same time somewhat relieved. I don't do smug, but if I did, now would be the time I imagine. I feel almost special but with ITP, I am anything but that.

The blood test nurse recognises me from my regular visits and I remember her because she always manages to draw my blood with minimal fuss and leave my arm bruise free. This is another sign that today might go well. I am told that I have veins which are difficult to locate. It had never crossed my mind but it is yet another thing I have learned from my ITP adventure. She routinely extracts the required samples and we laugh about how she takes more blood than Dracula. But it is difficult to escape the serious nature of her daily work. When all the samples are taken, labelled up and my puncture mark is covered we have a brief chat about my ITP. The nurse wishes me well and we conclude by saying that we hope we do not see each other again for ages.

By now I have been in the hospital for thirty minutes so I still have at least an hour to pass before I see my specialist, assuming he is on time with his appointments. This all fits nicely into my well drilled routine as it allows for the processing of my blood test and it permits me the luxury of getting refreshments from the coffee shop.

The barista at the coffee shop also recognises me. We chat about how we have been doing since my last visit to the hospital. All these familiar strangers that I meet at my clinic appointments are literally like clothes that you might have in your wardrobe but only wear now and again. The whole experience is as comfortable as it can possibly be because the wonderful people at the hospital make it so.

I have become a familiar face in an unfamiliar place as I saunter through my well rehearsed routine. I recognise most of the other patients waiting to be seen by the specialists today as I walk back to the waiting area of the clinic itself. I am grateful that so far my routine has played out exactly according to plan. One of the only things I cannot now control is how long the specialist will take to see the other patients booked in ahead of me. I am told that they are on time so far this morning. This is another good sign. I tell myself that if I am seen on time this is a good indication that my platelet numbers will be satisfactory. After all everything has gone smoothly this morning, the omens have been good so far. But of course the reality is that I cannot control that crucial platelet count, that arbitrary number which will determine the course my life takes from today.

I acknowledge the nervous signs from all the patients waiting to be seen by their respective specialists. I display those very same nervous signs too. We all try to read a newspaper, book or magazine. We all read the same sentence dozens of times. We all make sure at least ten times that our mobile phones are switched off. We all check the time every thirty seconds. We all hold back on any meaningful conversation because we cannot really discuss anything of any substance until after our appointments.

Any talk just has to be small and fairly cheap. It is impossible to think of anything meaningful or profound to say until we have had our fates read to us. Hopefully then the pressure valve will be released if the results are good. Sadly they will not be good for all of us and we all realise this as we await our respective consultations. Undoubtedly someone will go home with bad news. That I am afraid is the reality. We all hope that it is not going to be our turn to be disappointed, we pray that the bullet the specialist fires doesn't have our name on it. No wonder that we are all on edge.

It is now two minutes past eleven and I am looking at the examination room doors intently to see when my specialist will come out of his room. His door is number seven (my lucky number and surely another good sign). He is obviously running a bit late but that is not unusual. I convince myself that there is nothing to worry about even though my palms are not buying into that argument as they get ever stickier. I have cleaned them what seems like hundreds of times already with the antiseptic gel provided by the hospital to prevent the rampant spread of germs. But still I think I will need at least one more sanitising moment before seeing my specialist. It's just something else to do to pass the time.

At last the door to examination room seven squeaks open and my specialist comes down the corridor to greet me. He shakes my hand and ushers me into his room. I wonder if he has used the antiseptic hand gel as many times as I have ? He turns his computer screen towards me to show me the results of my blood test and the words he next uses confirm the good omens that my perfect routine had suggested. I really must buy a lottery ticket this afternoon.

My specialist explained that indeed it was really good news this morning as my platelet count was 112. The Rituximab treatment I had in July/August was obviously doing the trick. My platelet count had gone up from 63 on the day of my first infusion on July 16th. Whilst I understood it could lapse again at any time my specialist confirmed that for now I only need to see him three monthly for a check up, unless any symptoms re-appeared. Even better news was that I could stop taking Prednisolone immediately.

Those words confirmed that the omens had been good after all. For the time being at least, I had a platelet score 108 points higher than when I started out on this journey in July 2006. I know that remission is not redemption and it may only be a temporary reprieve. I understand that ITP will always be a part of me. I am stuck with it and it is stuck with me. We are each others' guilty secret. For now the omens had indeed been good and for a while, I could get back to living again.

So for the last quarter of 2010, you could say that I started to get my mojo back. My platelet counts stayed strong for the rest of the year, recording scores of 109 on September 21st, 133 on October 4th, 142 on November 1st and 132 on December 3rd. Although I had continued working ever since my ITP diagnosis in July 2006 and had tried to get on with life as normally as possible, it wasn't until I had Rituximab treatment that I really felt almost as good as my old self. Prednisolone and the wretched side effects coupled with the general uncertainties of the illness had simply meant that I was probably working a fair way short of my capacity.

So with a new sense of purpose and always looking for a new challenge, I decided in December 2010 to run for election to my local Town Council. The elections were due to take place in May 2011. I would never have even contemplated doing this before my Rituximab treatment. My general health, confidence in my platelet count and energy levels were simply not good enough. But with stable counts and feeling something like normal, my desire for a new challenge came back.

I had always been interested in politics and had been an active participant in local community issues. My working life was in financial services where I was a senior manager for a major British Bank. So it was quite natural for me to want to, at least have a look at local politics. I have also, never been shy when it comes to trying to help other people. I have always thrived on sharing knowledge and constantly seeking to challenge and be challenged. Anyway, for better or worse I was going to run for election and whatever happened I knew that it would be an interesting experience.

As my health was booming, I also wanted to find a way of getting involved with the ITP Support Association who had really helped me on my purple journey. I had become a member in 2008 but because my general health had been so unpredictable I had not as yet volunteered my services to them. To be honest I wasn't sure what I could do to help them. But I did know that trying to help them was something that would probably help me too. I have always believed that sharing a burden with others, talking about it and learning from other people is the only way any of us can really progress.

My first tentative involvement with the ITP Support Association came in January 2011. I was certain that writing up an article about my story to that point would be a useful place to start. It would hopefully be interesting for other purple people to read my case history. So I emailed an account of my ITP journey to Shirley Watson the founder of the ITP Support Association. Shirley confirmed that it would be published in the next edition of the quarterly magazine The Platelet. I had somehow managed to condense my 5 year ITP journey into an article of 2 pages.

Everything was going really well but in the past when my health seemed to be stable I was always suspicious that my old ITP ghost would come back to haunt me. But this time I was reasonably confident that I had got a welcome break from my ITP. I was fully aware that it could reawaken at any time but somehow, I was re- energised and more confident that I might get some lasting remission.

My confidence was endorsed on January 10th 2011 when my platelet count was 153 and my specialist confirmed that he would only see me every three months. No trips to the hospital apart from a quarterly check up. No parking hassles, taking time off work, anxious waiting for platelet counts to come back. It was a bit like finding that little stone that had been in your shoe all day and finally disposing of it. I could just get back to normal, I'd got a license to just BE.

I had started campaigning for the Town Council election which was to take place on Thursday May 5th and I was attending a lot of meetings with local community organisations. One key concern cropping up with local people was the decision that the Borough Council had made to consider privatising our libraries.

This would mean that our libraries would be run by a private company who no doubt would be seeking to do it for profit (why else would they do it ?) Ultimately our libraries would probably need to charge, introduce other revenue streams, close premises down and/or cut staff, facilities and assets. In a nutshell the prospect was that our library service would become another coffee shop with books.

Now I'm not unrealistic and I fully appreciated the very tight financial constraints we were being subjected to, BUT surely libraries are an investment not a cost ? As an advanced, civilised nation, one of the richest on the planet, surely we could provide a library service and see the benefit of doing it ? Couldn't we ? Well as it turned out the answer was a resounding YES. My colleagues and I organised a petition against privatising our local library service and it gained huge support and publicity. The local media got behind the campaign and the the plans for privatisation were shelved (no pun intended). It proves that if you care about it, you need to shout about it !

There were numerous other local issues that were really irritating people. The common denominator with all of them was that they were very small things we might assume are mundane. They are the things we rely on to keep our lives on track. These seemingly small things ARE the issues that get people ticking. It's the day to day stuff, the nitty-gritty if you like. So it's the trash collection, recycling, litter, graffiti, children's playing facilities, street lighting, litter bins, potholes in roads, local services like a Post Office, libraries, community centres all of these really matter.

On the ITP Support Association front, after a few emails with Shirley Watson, my wife and I found ourselves attending our first Annual Convention of the Association on April 16th. This was a great opportunity to meet fellow travellers on the purple journey and listen to presentations from some of the leading experts in ITP. The Convention was held at Wyboston Lakes in Bedfordshire and we learned so much from the various seminars..

For me the most important of the presentations was by Professor Julia Newton who talked about ITP and fatigue. Like most other ITP sufferers I had always felt that there was a link between my ITP and being very tired, almost completely exhausted. And yet, every specialist, nurse, doctor or health professional I had spoken to about it, basically dismissed it. Most ITP sufferers would have experienced the same response. So it was great to hear from Professor Newton that her research concluded that there was a link between fatigue and ITP .

The Convention provided a platform for all of us purple folk to share our ups and downs.The old saying that "a problem shared is a problem halved" seemed to sum up the whole experience for me. I suddenly realised that I wasn't fighting this thing alone and everything that had happened to me since July 2006 was hardly new. I was rare but hardly unique.

One other important development from that Convention was that I officially volunteered my services to the ITP Support Association. They had some really important events coming up in 2011 which needed some assistance. Shirley Watson confirmed that she would like me to be involved with something called ITP September Awareness Month. Shirley would email me details as soon as she had finalised some of the plans. Intrigued and pleased to be able to assist, I awaited her update.

My health continued to behave really well and my platelet count remained strong at 122 on April 4th. The only concern was that I did get quite a lot of headaches and very painful aching knees, ankles and elbow joints. My specialist reassured me that all of this was part of the withdrawal symptoms from the Prednisolone. There were days when I could barely move as my joints ached so much. But as I had so much to do, what with work, the Election coming up in May and some as yet unknown projects for the ITP Support Association in August/September, I really had to keep going.

Well, keep going I did and I learned so much from my local Town Council election campaign. It was interesting to be involved in local democracy. It was a real eye opener to get an understanding of what really concerns local people. I am very proud of the work we did to help save and ultimately expand our local library service. They are such an important community resource and contribute so much more than they ever cost. I was also delighted to see a clean up and anti graffiti team set up which to this day means we get virtually no unwanted budding Banksy's. We also have a local, volunteer litter picking team, which has nearly 300 members (including me) and it supplements the local council litter clearance teams.

But despite all these really positive initiatives, sadly I did not get elected to our local Town Council. I lost out by about 100 votes. At first the phrase .." it's not the winning, it's the taking part that counts" seemed hollow indeed. But I had never really appreciated that as a candidate standing for the first time, it was unlikely I would actually win on my debut.

The whole process was very interesting and a great eye opener. I met some incredible people throughout the campaign. There are so many amazing people of all political persuasions who work so hard, with real passion for the benefit of the local community, for little reward. Without them it is fair to say that all our lives would be poorer.

So after the set back of a defeat at the local Town Council election in May 2011, I really couldn't possibly have predicted that I would be making my debut speech in the House of Commons in September. But bizarrely, that is exactly what was about to happen.

CHAPTER TEN

Getting Social With Media and Speaking In The House

Throughout 2011 the Rituximab treatment that I had in July/August 2010 continued to work its' magic for me. For the first time since my ITP diagnosis in July 2006, I enjoyed a sustained period of good health, normal platelet counts and a general feeling of well being.

I was determined to make the most of this situation, knowing that my remission may or may not last. My specialist was very optimistic that as I had responded quickly to Rituximab it was a very good indicator that I would enjoy a sustained period of remission. He seemed confident that I would get at least 2 years remission. But of course he could not be certain. With ITP nobody ever can be !

Knowing that my remission period was not guaranteed, I was determined to make use of all the time that I had been given. As previously mentioned, I had already offered my services to the ITP Support Association. I'd had my ITP story published in their quarterly magazine The Platelet in March 2011. So I was intrigued when I received an email from Shirley Watson in June 2011 asking me to get involved in some very interesting activities they planned for September.

The activities that Shirley Watson mentioned were connected to the September ITP Annual Awareness Campaign. The amazing thing about ITP is that because it is so rare, it is just not really known about outside the ITP community. Even many health professionals, dentists and nurses that I had spoken to since my diagnosis were not familiar with our purple problem. I lost count of the number of times that I had to explain to people what ITP was, what the symptoms are and what dangers may befall ITP sufferers.

So anything that I could do to help in the September Awareness campaign I was more than willing to try. What I didn't know was that this would involve writing 3 articles for the press, making a training film about ITP for a pharmaceutical company, speaking in the House of Commons, then setting up the ITP Support Association on Facebook, TWITTER, LinkedIn and HealthUnlocked all within 3 months. But that is indeed the way things turned out and I enjoyed every minute of it.

As I had completed my Open University BA degree in 2008 and I was still studying some Social Sciences courses with them, I decided to write an article about my ITP for their regular *Platform* online magazine. As I have outlined in previous chapters, I had found my studies a great way to pass the wee small hours of my steroid induced sleepless nights. In many ways the goal of achieving my degree kept my mind on a positive course during my early purple years.

So I sent my article entitled …. *Immune Thrombocytopenia : Why Studying is a Welcome Distraction from Sleepless Nights*, to the Open University. On September 5th 2011, somewhat to my amazement, it was published just in time for the start of September Awareness month. This was really encouraging and gave me a tremendous boost. It pushed me to write another 2 articles for my local newspaper.

My local newspaper were equally obliging and actually very interested in my ITP story. They kindly published my articles *Shedding Light on a Mystery Condition* and then *Call **for** ITP Centres of Excellence* . So far, so good, though writing newspaper articles was one thing but making a training film was a whole different ball game. I had not really given much thought to what making a training film for a very large pharmaceutical group could actually involve. That was the next project on the horizon and whilst I knew that I was going to be involved in it, I had absolutely no clue what to expect.

Before attending the filming I had to sign a disclaimer about my involvement in the project and swear not to reveal anything to anybody about who the film was for. I began to think I might have to swallow any evidence. I had no idea exactly what they may want me to do. I thought they might just want me to have a chat and answer a few general ITP questions. A cup of tea, a digestive biscuit and a natter. No problem.

So on Monday September 12th I met Shirley Watson and her husband Frank at the secret, pre arranged location, details of which I am still, obviously precluded from revealing. We were greeted by a very welcoming group of people who included interviewers, camera crew, sound and lighting technicians and make up artists. In short, a film crew, armed with all the latest technology. Apparently we were also to face a lecture room full of delegates for an ITP Q and A after making the film too. No pressure then !

Well, although I had made a few training films during my career in financial services, and to be honest I had never really been daunted by any of it, this was a pretty eventful start to any Monday morning. Whilst our film was hardly Tarantino, Scorsese or Hitchcock, it was certainly suspense aplenty for the start of any week. But in for a penny and in for a pound as they say !

The filming was completed within about 3 hours and we were made to feel very comfortable throughout. The whole process was very enjoyable and the producers were very pleased with the end product. The point of the film was to explain what ITP was like from 2 perspectives. In my own case, they were interested in what it was like living day to day with ITP. On the other hand Shirley Watson gave a different view, as someone who had not only set up the ITP Support Association in 1995 but also, as a parent of an ITP sufferer. It was having a son with ITP that had led Shirley to establish the ITP Support Association in the first place.

So once the film was in the can and our make up removed, we were then ushered into a room full of about 30 delegates. The next hour was an ITP Q and A grilling, as the attendees asked us about everything purple. Our answers generated an interesting set of discussions, particularly about the nasty side effects of steroids, living day to day with ITP, and the mental anguish of not really knowing when, or if, our ITP might come or go or return again.

Following our silver screen efforts our attentions turned to an afternoon reception at the House of Commons on Thursday September 15th. The event was being hosted by Alistair Burt MP to mark ITP Awareness Month. The reception was in the magnificent Jubilee Room and in attendance were MP's, medical professionals, researchers, ITP sufferers and their families and some of the leading experts in ITP. So it was with a slight hint of trepidation that I set about writing a 10 minute speech that Shirley Watson had asked me to make to the gathering.

I had done quite a bit of public speaking in the past but obviously never in quite such lofty surroundings. My House of Commons debut, so to speak, was to be an account of my ITP story to date. So it was a matter of condensing 5 purple years into 10 minutes.
No easy task but all the same 10 minutes is actually much longer than anyone can really imagine once you get on your feet and look out onto a sea of expectant faces.

I was one of 4 speakers telling our own version of purple events as each of us explained our unique path along the ITP road. More than anything else it showed that nothing about ITP is definite, the illness can come to people of all ages, for different reasons. Our responses to the many treatments are as varied as the British weather and there is absolutely no one size fits all advice about treatments. What suits one, will not suit another. What gives serious side effects to one, will often not trouble another. In our 4 presentations we each bore witness to the fickle nature of our illness and the variable responses to the treatments on offer.

The House of Commons reception was a really enjoyable experience, although it was a little daunting until I got my 10 minute speech out of the way. In rather dramatic surroundings, with a very celebrated audience we had really made great strides in helping to spread ITP awareness. Once our gathering had broken up it was then a great pleasure to have a tour of the Palace of Westminster. I had been fortunate enough to have seen quite a bit of it in the past but I never tire of drinking in the Gothic majesty of the rebuilt seat of Government.

Looking back on that September awareness campaign, I was pleased that I had been able to contribute 3 ITP articles to the press, taken part in a video training film for a major pharmaceutical company and spluttered through a 10 minute House of Commons speech about my ITP. All this in the space of 2 weeks.

I was under no illusions that without having had successful Rituximab treatment in July/August 2010, I could never have done these things, half as well. If I had stayed on Prednisolone I don't think I would have been able to do myself or anyone else full justice. I was very fortunate that Rituximab had worked for me, grateful that it was continuing to work for me but nevertheless uncertain whether or not it would continue to keep me purple free.

One thing that I was certain about was that I was due to make some important announcements in early October. This was because Shirley Watson had asked me to set up the ITP Support Association on the main social media outlets and maintain regular communication on them.

So Facebook, Twitter, LinkedIn and HealthUnlocked were to be my windows on the ITP world. I didn't know then that it would lead me to write my own ITP blog and subsequently this book but in September 2011 there were still so many things about ITP and my purple journey that I still hadn't discovered.

Since starting the social media forums I have been delighted with the positive feedback from so many members, followers and friends. It has been a hugely successful venture and it is so beneficial to share experiences with fellow sufferers. Ultimately we are the people who really know what ITP is like. The purple spectre is constantly hanging over us and it is so helpful to be able to share that burden with other ITP folk.

Returning to the hospital for my next check up, my platelet count measured 144 on November 14th 2011 and it had been well over 100 since my Rituximab treatment in Summer 2010. My overall health was very good and it got me wondering about the flu jab. I had never had the flu jab at all, either pre purple or since. But my wife has it every winter because she is asthmatic. So my usual inquisitive nature got me thinking about whether I should have it or not.

As usual with everything ITP, there is no definite answer regarding whether or not to have the flu jab. It is each case on its' merits, and there are many factors to consider before deciding what is best for each individual. So my specialist discussed the flu jab with me and our conversation was structured around the following questions.....

1.What type of work do you do ? Is it office based or in a job where you may be in contact with lots of people, so potentially exposure to flu's, colds, viruses is higher ?

2.How do you get to work? Do you commute on a packed train or London Underground for example ? If this is the case, you may be more vulnerable to illnesses.

3.Do you have any other medical conditions ? Asthma, bronchitis, diabetes, heart problems.

4.Do you take any other medication and what other medications have you taken in the past ? So for people like me who had taken immune suppressing drugs this was very important, as we would be more vulnerable to catching everything and anything.

5.Have you got any children as they also tend to bring viruses, colds, flu's home from school quite often ? Do you work with children, teaching, lecturing, child minding?

6.Do you work long hours, night shifts ? This might weaken your resilience to flu, viruses, infections etc.

7.Do you eat a healthy diet ? Make sure it contains plenty of fresh fruit and vegetables and do you drink plenty of water ?

8.Age... the older you are, the more vulnerable you are.

As I seemed to fall into a relatively low risk category as far as being likely to contract flu, I decided not to have the flu jab. I do not work in an office and I am fortunate to work most of the time from home. I do not have any train journeys or London Underground or buses to endure and I have nothing but my ITP for medical trouble. So on balance I decided that my flu risk was pretty low but as ever with ITP I re-emphasise that we are all different. It is a decision for each individual to do what they feel is best after discussing it in full with their specialist.

As we ended 2011, my general health, my platelets, my well being, and outlook were as good as they had been since before my purple days began. I couldn't wait for 2012 because it was an Olympic year and London, my home City, would be hosting the summer games and Paralympics. As a self confessed sports nut and a Londoner born and bred, what more could I possibly want ? Well what about Rare Disease day for starters?

In February of 2012 I was invited by Shirley Watson to represent the ITP Support Association at the Rare Disease Day event at the beautiful Royal Holloway College. It was the beginning of my involvement with the annual campaign. My Rare Disease Day debut in 2012 was a great start to what would turn out to be a very eventful year. I ended up going for Gold but soon I would sadly take my next purple tumble .

CHAPTER ELEVEN

Going for Gold at London 2012 but Heading For A Fall

The doom mongers and nay sayers in the UK had always predicted that London 2012 would be a disaster of Titanic proportions. But sadly for them, yet wonderful for the rest of us, it was actually an Olympic sized success. Something seems to happen to us folk in little old Blighty when we are told we can't do something or won't do it well. That's when we seem to find one of our finest hours !

We usually seem to get the big stuff right, especially if it includes music, a bit of pomp, dressing up in strange costumes and engaging in some generally understated showing off. It's a pity the simple things often give us grief. But from the moment that Her Majesty the Queen and James Bond parachuted into the London Olympic stadium on Friday night, July 27th to open the Games, we knew we were in safe hands. Even the usually unpredictable British weather held good. My general health and platelets were excellent throughout 2012 too and looking back on that period it was probably one of the most settled and enjoyable of my purple years.

Now I won't spoil things too much but when purple things are going well, ITP sufferers will know that you are skating on thinnish ice. I have already highlighted this many times in previous chapters. So as I well knew, quite often a platelet fall, a random bruise or something unwelcome makes an appearance just when you least expect it. But I promised not to spoil things so for the moment let's just say that 2012 went as well for me as it did for Team GB. As for 2013, that's another story.

On February 24th 2012 I attended the first of many Rare Disease UK events on behalf of the ITP Support Association. The occasion was part of the annual Rare Disease Day schedule and was held at the rather splendid Royal Holloway College in Egham, Surrey. It was great to meet representatives from other small, rare disease charities. These amazing people work tirelessly, usually voluntarily, on behalf of their members, who like us purple folk, suffer from rare, often unheard of illnesses.

The event demonstrated to me just how many rare illnesses there are. Some of them, including ITP, are suffered by quite small numbers of people. But as a whole, rare diseases actually affect very high numbers of people. A rare disease is defined by the European Union as one that affects less than 5 in 10,000 of the general population. There are between 6,000 and 8,000 known rare diseases and around five new rare diseases are described in medical literature each week.

About 1 in 17 people, or 7% of the population, will be affected by a rare disease at some point in their lives. This equates to about 3.5 million people in the UK and 30 million people across Europe. In the UK, a single rare disease may affect up to about 30,000 people. But the vast majority of rare diseases will affect far fewer than this – some will impact only a handful, or even a single person in the UK. Sadly, 75% of rare diseases affect children. Rare diseases include rare illnesses such as childhood cancers and some other well known conditions, such as cystic fibrosis and Huntington's disease.

In ITP about four in every 100,000 children develop it each year. It is more common in girls than boys. Many children, particularly younger ones, suddenly improve within six weeks, whether or not treatment has been given. Three out of four children will have improved by 6 months after the start of their ITP. In adults ITP is much more stubborn and does not as easily fall into remission even when treated.

Having attended the Rare Diseases Day event at Royal Holloway College it gave me a great sense of confidence knowing that although ITP is a rare illness, we are not the only rare condition. We are not alone in our fight either, because we have each other, we have our individual patient groups like the ITP Support Association, but we also have the terrific support of Rare Disease UK and Europe wide there is Eurordis. The important thing is to get behind the work they do, because it's the only way our rare voices get heard. If you don't shout no one will hear you. It is completely free to join Rare Disease UK by the way, and you can do so via https://www.raredisease.org.uk

Meanwhile the road to the London 2012 Olympics was getting shorter and shorter and despite the pessimism of some, the Olympic Games in London were magnificent, widely recognised as probably the most successful ever. It was brilliant to be involved in just a small part of the project and exciting to go along to some of the events. I will never forget the incredible, feel good factor that was evident up and down our country during that time. Everything went smoothly and the successes across so many events for Team GB kept the nation gripped.

It was very difficult to believe that all the planning and immense effort exerted on the London 2012 Games was over so quickly but as always, all good things must come to an end. The week after the Paralympic Games ended, my wife and I took a welcome break to Bruges in Belgium. We had a lovely holiday eating too much chocolate, too many mussels and drinking sensible amounts of beer. It was also wonderful taking in some of the beautiful medieval architecture and more soberly visiting some of the battlefield sites of WW1.

Both my Grandfathers had served in the army in WW1 and both somehow survived the horrors of the Ypres salient. Like so many, they were still just teenagers when they enlisted. They'd never even left England until being despatched to Belgium in 1915. So I had always wanted to see for myself, some part of what they saw and in some sense get at least a small connection with some of the experiences they had.

Visiting the City of Ypres, the Menin Gate, Sanctuary Wood and Tyne Cot Cemetery were some of the most sobering moments of my life. It is almost incomprehensible to imagine just how awful the war must have been. The sheer scale of the losses on all sides, the noise, the mud, the vermin, the disease. Then there are the huge numbers of men who were never found, the terrible wounds and the psychological damage.

Perhaps the most astounding thing about it all is that they were so young and from literally every corner of the globe. We had always known all of this but to see it up close is literally overwhelming. It's unbelievable how bad it really must have been. Sadly, just under 21 years after WW1, conflict would break out again and even further horrors would descend upon the world. It would be my Father's turn to serve in the army in 1939 and somehow survive horrors that no teenager should witness.

We shed a few tears on that Belgian trip and I don't think any human being could avoid doing so. It was a very humbling experience and made my own ITP problems, seem like very small beer. I fully appreciate that our trip to Belgium may seem a long way from ITP, but seeing some of the horrific realities of war puts things like ITP in perspective. All too often in our cosseted modern world, we forget just how lucky we are. Even if we are purple victims we have to remember that in most cases our ITP can be controlled. It certainly reminded me to remain positive about things, whether they be purple issues or the daily trivia we all have to sort out.

Returning to the UK I was given a wonderful boost on October 22nd when my platelet count was still flying high at 135. I was dismissed from the hospital and my specialist confirmed that he would not need to see me again for a further six months. Would my platelet count and general health still be good by the time I saw him again on April 16th 2013 ?

The London 2012 Olympic Games had been an overwhelming success and a good platelet year for me too. My general health was very good but there was definitely an "after the Lord Mayor's show " feeling once the Olympic circus had left town. Nevertheless, I started 2013 in a very positive frame of mind.

On February 27th 2013 my wife and I attended the Rare Disease Day House of Commons reception organised by Rare Disease UK. The event was hosted by Liz Kendall MP for Leicester West and Shadow Junior Health Minister. Other speakers were The Earl Howe, Parliamentary under Secretary of State for Quality at the Department of Health, Alastair Kent OBE, Chair of Rare Disease UK and Director of Genetic Alliance and Professor Bobby Gaspar, Professor of Paediatrics and Immunology at Great Ormond Street Hospital.

In the early part of 2013 my own health seemed to be good and I had no idea that I was heading for a fall. As we know, time and time again, this is one of the problems with ITP. It is almost impossible to predict when your platelets are going to start causing trouble. I started the year believing that my count was pretty good, albeit the only actual count I could rely on was 135 on October 22nd 2012. The next check up I had was on April 16th 2013 and my count had fallen by then to 66.

Having seen my count fall to 66 my specialist was very honest with me and said that he believed they were going to fall right back to single figures, probably within about a month or so. I was due to attend the ITP Support Association Annual Convention on April 20th at the Chateau Impney Hotel in Droitwich but my specialist advised me to rest and take no unnecessary risks. He felt that my platelets were going to plummet and he turned out to be right. He suggested that we wait for a couple of weeks before starting any treatment. Furthermore he felt that as Rituximab had given me over 2 years of remission it would be worth having a further round of It. He was very optimistic I would respond well again and get at least a similar purple free period.

It seemed almost inevitable that my platelet count had fallen to 27 by May 14th and to avoid any further risk my specialist got me started on Rituximab treatment as soon as possible. The first time that I'd had Rituximab in July 2010 it was fair to say that I was more than a little apprehensive. But this time I was very calm about it and very optimistic that it would get my platelets back up to normal levels. So I was almost as cool as Cary Grant in a Hitchcock thriller when I reported for my Rituximab treatment on May 26th 2013.

The routine was exactly as it had been on my first Rituximab journey back in July 2010. The treatment I had on May 26th took about 7 hours. Just like my Rituximab experience in 2010 during the first of the four doses, I got a very sore/scratchy throat and tightness in my breathing and a rash across my chest , after about an hour. The treatment was stopped for an hour and then once it proceeded I got no further problems. Once again the treatment was done very slowly.

It was a very long 7 hours of watching a very expensive drug dribble into my arm. The minute hand on the clock on the wall was deliberately dragging, ignoring the laws of time. Every minute seemed like an hour but at no time was I concerned. The main issue was the fact that I had to keep fairly still for such a long period. I'm not good at lazing around and doing nothing. I just can't rest easy unless I am doing something useful or constructive.

The trouble is that when you've got your left arm strapped to a wobbly hat stand contraption which is feeding a fairly serious drug into your body, you can't really move very far. Whatever movements you make can never look elegant or remotely coordinated. If you should need to go to the bathroom you see grown men and women running for cover as you spin around like a supermarket trolley on wonky wheels. I can laugh at it all now but at the time it was decidedly hazardous.

The good news was that my platelets responded well. When I reported back for my 2nd dosage my count had gone up from 27 to 45. The second dosage took much less time than the first and within 5 hours I was finished. Subsequently the 3rd and 4th infusions also went very smoothly both taking about 4 hours to complete. The really good news was that once my 4th and final dosage was completed my platelet count had increased to 58. By June 26th my count had rocketed to 78 and then by July 24th it was 101

So Rituximab seemed to have worked well for me again and I did not have any noticeable reaction or side effects from it. By August 19th my count had reached 117 and then on November 19th it was at 122. This very welcome stability made me feel quite optimistic. Perhaps I could look forward to a similar period of remission with this latest round of Rituximab as I'd had from my treatment in Summer 2010. I had enjoyed 2 years and 8 months purple free, so hopefully I might be granted something similar or better this time.

The rest of 2013 passed without any further ITP troubles so I had every reason to be positive about 2014 as I looked ahead to the launch of a special fundraising campaign for the ITP Support Association. We were embarking on a year long mission to raise funds to build a new headquarters completely from scratch. The project would hopefully be completed by Summer 2015 in time to coincide with the 20th anniversary of the founding of the ITP Support Association.

As I looked ahead to 2014, I couldn't possibly have predicted what my purple enemy was going to throw at me next. But by the Spring I would be the victim of another unexpected ITP ambush and yet another unpleasant episode.

Chapter Twelve

Walking On The Wild Side

So thankfully, my second Rituximab encounter in May/June 2013 seemed to produce very similar results to my debut with that drug in Summer 2010. By February 25th 2014 my platelet count had settled at 136, having been above 100 since July 2013.

My wife and I were fortunate enough to attend the Rare Disease Day House of Commons reception on February 26th, with the theme for the event being - *Join Together for Better Care*. The focus was on drawing attention to the different types of care that rare disease sufferers need. Some patients require highly sophisticated, intense, complex treatments and care, whilst others need relatively simple assistance. Whatever the needs of the individual the important thing is that provision is made by Governments, health professionals and associated agencies with detailed, strategic plans.

The House of Commons reception was once again hosted by Liz Kendall MP, who has been a great supporter of Rare Disease campaigns over many years, as has Earl Howe who once again attended the 2014 event as a guest speaker.

I was full of optimism and enjoying good health with near normal platelet levels, so what could possibly go wrong ? Well, as usual with ITP, just when you think everything is going well, and of course just when you have got something important planned...... BOOM !!! The purple hand grenade gets thrown and chaos ensues. So in March 2014, almost inevitably, ITP ambushed me just when I thought my health had settled down. It couldn't have been worse as it was only days before I was due to attend the ITP Support Association Annual Convention in Letchworth.

The Convention was due to take place on Saturday April 5th and a week before , completely unprovoked and totally out of the blue, my right knee and my right ankle became very swollen, very painful and angrily red. I literally couldn't stand up or even move without assistance. So, now what ? Where had this come from, what on earth was it this time and how long would I be incapacitated ? For the entire week I was in complete agony and I was also getting very hot and feverish. I was just so uncomfortable and in truth, absolutely sick of being sick.

I somehow managed to take enough Paracetamol to dull down the pain from my knee and ankle so that my wife and I could attend the Convention. But although I made a big effort to engage with fellow sufferers and the many ITP experts attending, I was really struggling. Yet again my ITP had almost stolen the show albeit I would never allow it to beat me. Even having to go through the weekend as Long John Silver, I was determined to carry on with my plans. I was walking or at least limping and shuffling on the wild side but I'd still learned so much from the Convention. I had still won !

The ITP Support Association Convention was as ever, a hugely important opportunity to meet up with fellow purple people and learn from each other as well as get up to date information from some of the leading experts. The guest speakers at the 2014 event were Dr Nichola Cooper from Hammersmith Hospital, Dr John Grainger from Manchester Children's Hospital, Professor John Hunter from Addenbrooke's Hospital and Professor James George from the University of Oklahoma.

I found that the presentation by Professor George rang lots of bells with me, as he discussed the psychological impact of being an ITP sufferer. During my journey I had felt that the mental tests were almost as troublesome as the blood tests. Having unpredictable health had certainly undermined my overall confidence as well as reducing my concentration levels and productive capacity. I suppose it also starts you thinking about your own mortality and it just seems to wear you down. But it also made me even more determined and resourceful.

Amazingly on May 29th my platelet count was 137 which surprised me as I had thought that due to the swollen knee and ankle episode in March/April, I might see a fall. The limping had gone on for about 2 weeks in total but everything then just went back to normal. It was as if nothing had really happened. When I explained this to my specialist he could not really give a definite answer as to what had happened. He said that it might be linked to the long periods of steroid usage I'd had from 2006 to 2010. I'd had a similar attack in August 2009 but I've not had anything like it since 2014 and I am grateful for that.

So with my platelets high and general health seemingly restored my wife and I decided to make the most of it. We took a week away to the lovely town of Whitstable, Kent. Although it was not oyster season, which the town is famous for, we still enjoyed plenty of other great seafood. I had stayed in the town as a student back in the stone ages (late 1970's) when I was at Kent University and I'd always wanted to go back and browse around. I'd also always wanted to visit Pugin's Grange in Ramsgate and the Turner Contemporary Margate. So we managed to fit quite a lot into that week of June 9th 2014. The wretched memories of my agonising limp in Spring already seemed an age ago.

My platelet count on September 29th 2014 was a normal 155 and I wasn't required to have any further check up's until early January 2015. I had no other health issues, seemingly no other side effects from the Rituximab I'd had in June 2013. All was well but as ever the next mini crisis was just around the corner. How many times have I had to use that phrase or something similar during this book ?

With ITP, we all want to hear something beautiful but mostly just have to settle for the awkward truth. In the main, the truth is that ITP is uncertain, it is confusing, it is awkward, it is unpredictable, it is annoying, it is Idiopathic....the clue is in the name. It's the mosquito that you hear buzzing around your room when the lights are turned off, but then disappears once the lamp is switched back on.

The next purple problem for me was yet another thing that I'd never heard of. But in January 2015 I was quickly going to learn about it. Ever heard of platelet clumping ? No, well nor had I but don't worry, in the next few pages I can tell you all about it.

By 2015 I had become something of an old timer with ITP. I had long ago accepted that denial of the illness might dull the pain of it but that would never remove the causes or provide a cure. I had also realised that occasionally, a short blast of inclement ITP weather can strike across the bows. It's almost a reminder that ITP demands attention just when you are beginning to think you can ignore it. The wasp at a picnic analogy is one I've used before in this book and to be honest it is still the best description I can think of. It is a wholly unwanted guest at an otherwise enjoyable event. It never gets the message that you want it to go away and it has a habit of buzzing around you when you think it has gone.

So it was that in January 2015, I encountered yet another blast of an ITP storm in the form of clumping platelets. Until this strange and unexpected element hit me I had never heard of it before. Like ITP itself it knocked me completely off course until I managed to get it explained to me. I had thought that everything was going well as my last platelet count was 155 at the end of September 2014 and had been consistently over 100 since my Rituximab treatment in June 2013.

The first time I heard the phrase clumping platelets, was on January 26th 2015 following my routine blood test on January 15th. I got a telephone cal from the hospital advising me that the blood test I'd had was inconclusive. They couldn't actually get a definite platelet count from it because my platelets (God love them) had clumped.

This was a complete bolt from the blue and it took the wind out of my sails just a bit. Clumping platelets are actually quite common and to the health professionals they are easy to understand. But to us ordinary folk it is disconcerting and almost incomprehensible until we get it explained in plain language. I suppose that is the case with so much about ITP and indeed many illnesses.

So in a slightly apprehensive mood, I returned to the hospital on January 28th to get another blood test, hoping that this time I would not clump. On arrival the senior nurse explained that platelet clumping is quite common, albeit in my own case I'd never had it before in my 9 purple years to date. She reassured me that although my blood test of January 15th did not return a conclusive platelet count, my specialist had analysed the blood sample manually and estimated that my count was over 100. So to an extent that settled my anxiety somewhat, as clearly I was safe for the time being. But nonetheless I was curious about this clumping thing.

My curiosity grew further when the blood test that I had on January 28th was also inconclusive, as my platelets had clumped again. Once more my specialist analysed that blood sample manually and confirmed that he could see plenty of platelets and estimated that my count was still well over 100. Exactly the same happened with yet another blood test on February 4th. Curious indeed.

So what exactly is platelet clumping and why does it occur ? That was basically what I wanted to know and understand. Who else could I ask for a plain English answer than the ITP Support Association where, as ever, Shirley Watson got the reassuring explanation that settled my nerves. A very straight forward description of clumping platelets was provided by Professor Jim George from the ITP Support Association medical panel.

The way I understand platelet clumping is that when a blood test is done a chemical is routinely used in the test tube on the blood sample. The chemical used in most cases is EDTA (Ethylenediamientetraacetic Acid) . Sometimes, as happened in my case in January and February 2015, platelets clump in the test tube when EDTA is used. So sort of understandable but nevertheless still curious. I kept wondering why it had never happened to me before in over 9 years and probably hundreds of blood tests. I asked this very question of my specialist but he simply could not say.

Blood samples can be tested using different chemicals to get a platelet count, so if EDTA gives an inconclusive result because of clumping other chemicals can be employed in the blood test to get a count. So when I had yet another blood test on February 24th I had 3 samples taken. One of the samples was to be tested with EDTA, the second to be tested in Citrate (an alternative chemical) and the third to be tested using Lithium Heparin (yet another chemical). The results came back completely satisfactory this time, showing a platelet count of 139 and amazingly they did not clump in the EDTA.

At a subsequent follow up blood test on March 6th, again I provided 3 samples to be tested with the 3 different chemicals as I had done on February 24th. Once again the results were clear, the EDTA solution did not give clumping platelets and I returned a count of 125. Another blood test on April 28th using the EDTA solution gave me a platelet count of 159 and again no clumping issues. In fact the clumping platelet problem did not resurface ever again and has not been an issue for me since,

My personal view is that in January/February 2015, the laboratory carrying out the blood tests at my hospital must have been doing either 1) something different or 2) not doing something they had previously been doing or 3) they may have even doing something incorrectly compared to previous years. It is a very strange coincidence that after 9 years of ITP , numerous blood tests and check up's, I had never clumped before, and indeed apart from January/February 2015, I never clumped again. The whole thing remains a mystery ...The Curious Case of the Clumping Platelets.

Despite the clumping issues, my platelet count actually remained good for the whole of 2015 and I got no purple symptoms. What I did get was a period of awful headaches, palpitations and terrible anxiety. I went to my doctor in March and I had a check up. Everything appeared to be fine, although she felt that the whole clumping platelet episode may have triggered off anxiety, hence the headaches, palpitations and heart burn. The advice was to get some rest and relaxation, get on with life as normal. Easier said than done of course.

So quite a nervy start to 2015 but despite everything I carried on, carrying on. I attended the Rare Disease Day House of Commons Reception on February 25th, once again hosted by MP Liz Kendall. The theme for the event was *Living with a Rare Disease* and as far as I'm concerned this got to the very heart of the matter. Focusing on what it is really like day to day for us rare disease sufferers conveys the reality of our story (s). Only we, the sufferers know what we are really going through. It is only we who fully appreciate the physical, mental & financial, constraints that our illness imposes not just on us but on our friends, families, and work colleagues.

On March 17th, it was great to forget about my clumping platelets for an evening when we went to see my old school friends *Spandau Ballet* at the O2 Arena, London. It was nice to see them playing live again and enjoying their music. It followed a prolonged and quite acrimonious legal battle, which tore them apart. It's sad that they had to go through it but watching them at the O2 Arena that night, they just looked relieved to get back to playing music.

For the rest of 2015, after the platelet clumping, things went very well. I was blessed with good counts all year and we had some great musical highlights including, Cecile McLorin

Salvant, Lizz Wright, Lance Ellington and Curtis Stagers all at Ronnie Scott's, Joe Stilgoe in *High Society* at the Old Vic, plus Ian Shaw and Anthony Strong at Pizza Express Soho.

On Saturday September 19th the new ITP Support Association HQ was opened by actor Neil Dudgeon and it was the culmination of a huge fundraising effort by so many people. It was due to the efforts of so many wonderful volunteers, contributors and fund raisers that at last the ITP Support Association had a permanent, purpose built home. After 20 years based in a spare out building of founder Shirley Watson MBE, the charity now had a home base of its' own.

A great majority of the new HQ was constructed by Frank Watson, Shirley Watson and a host of volunteers. They were the very essence of the "if you build it they will come" spirit. The new ITP Support Association HQ is called The Platelet Mission and I think that is highly appropriate. A huge thank you goes to the many people involved in the fund raising and construction project.

I was very proud to have contributed by promoting all of the various activities on the ITP Support Association social media platforms as well as having been involved in the original planning meetings for the project in 2013/14. It was so satisfying to see the new HQ open for business and putting the charity of a firm footing for the future.

Throughout the year, we had been determined that the purple menace would not get in the way if we could possibly help it. Overall, 2015 had been pretty stable platelet wise. Even though the curious case of the clumping platelets had diverted us for a while, life had to go on. But as ever with ITP in February 2016, I was to discover another moment when you know, that you know, that you know, that something is wrong.

CHAPTER THIRTEEN

The Moment You Know, You Know, You Know

For us ITP folk there are certain moments in our individual purple journey's that become etched in our memories. I'm sure most of us remember the date when we were diagnosed or perhaps the date we gained remission if we have been lucky enough to achieve it. Well for me an equally memorable date is Saturday February 6th 2016. I can even remember an exact time .... 8pm .... It is the moment that I knew, that I knew, that I knew, my ITP had returned again. Somehow my inner Dr Jekyll could sense the re - appearance of the cunning, purple Mr Hyde.

When my appointment with my latest relapse eventually came it was at just over an hour since I had been watching England Rugby win 15 points to 9 against Scotland, in what was to turn out to be the first leg of a 6 Nations Grand Slam. Well completely out of the blue, and totally unprovoked my right hand developed a tell tale purple bruise. The all too familiar ITP tattoo. Mr Hyde was back in play.

Undoubtedly this was the moment that I knew it was back. The ITP jack had well and truly sprung from its' box AGAIN. Despite trying to explain the huge bruise away as a possible accident from earlier in the day, my wife and I both knew that it could be nothing else but the return of our unwelcome enemy. I suppose I should have known it as I'd been feeling quite tired over the last few weeks. But it was not just tired, it was sting like a butterfly, float like a stone, levels of fatigue. A sure sign that a purple storm was brewing.

So off my wife and I trundled to the Royal Berkshire Hospital first thing on the Monday morning February 8th at 8am. We had contemplated reporting to A and E on the Saturday evening but as I had not had any other symptoms apart from the bruise we decided to just take things easy on the Saturday evening and Sunday, then report on the Monday first thing. We both knew what the outcome was going to be. We had trodden this same path many times over the last ten years and we arrived at the hospital with weary resignation.

A blood test revealed that my platelet count was only 20 and that it had fallen from 100 since my last test only 2 weeks ago. So it was no wonder that I had started to bruise. The next step was yet another round of Prednisolone treatment to get my platelet count back to safe levels. I had always responded very quickly to steroid treatment in the past, so we were reasonably confident that I would do so again. This would be my 5th steroid encounter in my ITP journey.

So it was back on the familiar Prednisolone horse at 85mg per day accompanied by 20mg of Omeprazole. We ITP sufferers know that the problem with the old steroid nag is that it is never a favourite because of the truly awful side effects. It might eventually get you round the course but it certainly hits most of the fences around the track. Anyway, my Platelet count responded really well and increased to 141 after the first week.

However it wasn't the only thing to increase. My waist, my body mass index, my blood pressure, my chins, my weight, the speed with which I ate, the amount of food I consumed, my temper, my mood swings, my headaches, my waking up in the early hours of the morning all made unwanted gains as they are prone to do when on the steroid. Sounds familiar !

At the outset of this round of steroid treatment I made it quite clear to my specialist that I would only go back on the Prednisolone short term. This was just to get my platelet levels safe and then we would look at other treatment options. He agreed with my view and suggested the following options for our consideration....

1) Another round of Rituximab, 2) Mycophenolate Mofetil (MMF), 3) Eltrombopag, 4) N-Plate. These options were just an initial list and obviously much depended on how quickly or even if my count responded to the steroid.

Fortunately my platelet count responded well, albeit with a few blips along the way. Anyway by April 21st my platelet levels had stabilised at consistently around the 150 mark and my steroid dosage had gradually been tapering down. Now was the time to strike while the iron was hot and sneak in my new anti ITP weapon. My specialist and my wife and I had a good discussion about what to do and when to do it.

Now was the time for Mychophenolate Mofetil (MMF) to be introduced. In addition to full discussions with my specialist I also took the opportunity to get my case referred to the ITP Support Association medical panel. I am so grateful to Shirley Watson for doing this for me and to all the advice offered by the panel. Ultimately however, we all have to make up our own minds about how to proceed but it sure helps to have excellent information to help you make the decision.

For those not familiar with it, MMF is another immune suppressing drug which looks to raise the platelet count by slowing down the destruction of platelets. It hopefully achieves this by suppressing the immune system and its' penchant for incorrectly attacking and destroying our platelets. It has the added benefit in most cases, of fewer nasty side effects. But as usual we have to emphasise that we all respond differently to all these treatments and all encounter different side effects to varying degrees.

The MMF, like Rituximab can take 2 to 3 months to impact on the platelet count so it is important to coordinate it with any existing treatment holding the platelet count safe. So the idea for me, was to start the MMF whilst still on the steroid albeit at a reducing Prednisolone dosage. We hoped that whilst the MMF was taking hold the steroid would prop up the platelet count. This strategy commenced on April 23rd and I started on 750 mg of MMF twice a day. The steroid dosage slowly reduced by sensible increments each fortnight until June 25th when I stopped all Prednisolone. The Omeprazole stopped 2 weeks later.

My platelet count was 169 at my blood test on July 26th. I'd had no bruising or any other symptoms since the initial bruise I got back on February 6th. I was to remain on 750 mg of MMF twice a day and no other medication. The only side effects I had were more to do with withdrawing from the steroid (I think), than taking the MMF. I suppose with the overlap of medication it is difficult to say for sure which drug was the culprit. I suffered terrible head aches, cramp in my legs and feet, hot sweats and achy knees and legs once I stopped taking the steroid. These subsequently stopped about 2 to 3 months after ending the steroid dosage.

I was delighted to see the back of the steroid once more. Unless absolutely desperate I will not ride that horse ever again. This time on the steroid I seemed to be less tolerant of it and I vowed that I would not put myself or my wife through it again. Hopefully the MMF would continue to prop up my platelets, without any side effects. Only time would tell, but meanwhile I was now to be checked only quarterly at the hospital. My next challenge was to get my weight, waist, BMI and diet back under control, and lose a couple of my chins.

With a very stable platelet count, courtesy of MMF, I was delighted to attend the annual ITP Support Association Convention on September 17th. As usual, it was a great opportunity to catch up with fellow ITP sufferers and draw on each others' good, bad and ugly experiences. As I have mentioned before, it is only when you discuss your illness with other people who are going through the same things, that you really find that you are not as unique as you think that you are. Nothing that I had experienced was ever new, and just hearing that other people had trodden the same path was and continues to be such a huge boost.

The Convention was held at The Cumberwell Golf Club , Bradford-On -Avon, near the beautiful city of Bath. We were treated to presentations from some of the leading experts in ITP. Professor Godeau started off the day with his lecture on refractory ITP patients. Dr Angharad Care delivered a presentation on ITP and pregnancy. The next session was from Dr Will Lester on primary versus secondary ITP. The afternoon then proceeded with Dr Drew Provan giving an update on the latest ITP developments, treatments and research.

The whole day was yet another reminder of how important it is to get involved in these events. The annual Convention is open to anyone with any interest in ITP and if you can possibly get along to one, then you will not regret it. The information, support and sharing of knowledge and experiences are priceless. To find details of the annual Convention, the ITP Support Association website is the place to look. You do not have to be a member of the Association to attend the Convention, so if you haven't been to one, do try to get to the next event.

As I came to the end of 2016 and what had been quite a traumatic year, even by purple standards, I could take some consolation from my last platelet count being 152 on November 7th. The side effects that I'd had from MMF were slight nausea, tummy upset, general indigestion and slight difficulty sleeping. Just like Prednisolone, the MMF has a habit of disturbing sleep patterns but as we know, nothing is perfect in ITP world. Also in the same way that Prednisolone, Azathioprine, Rituximab and other immune suppressing drugs, leave the patient much more vulnerable to colds, flus, infections, viruses, the MMF lowers our resistance to such illnesses.

It is so important to be careful to avoid situations where colds, flus, viral infections may be easily spread. It is extremely difficult to avoid every potential problem but I am certainly more aware of some very simple things that help to keep illness at bay. I try to avoid getting into crowded places, especially elevators, trains, buses, the London Underground. This is extremely difficult but I try to plan my journeys outside the peak times when it is busy with bigger crowds. I am fortunate that my work allows me flexibility about arranging meetings to suit my situation.

In many discussions with fellow ITP patients at various meetings and on the numerous online platforms, I have had lots of debate and suggestions about alternative remedies, herbal treatments for colds, flus, viruses and even ITP itself. The first thing to say is that I personally have never tried anything other than conventional medicines prescribed to me by my specialists. I will highlight the many reasons why I personally have opted to tread this path.

It is certainly not my intention to criticise any fellow ITP sufferers for trying any alternative options. Why wouldn't we all at least be interested in learning about anything that would tackle the purple riddler? It is bound to pique our interest especially for those who have tried numerous conventional treatments without any success. In such circumstances the lure of trying something off piste might be very tempting.

All that said, the following important factors are the ones that I considered to be key in persuading me not to try any alternative treatments including things like Papaya Leaf extract and Aloe Vera juice.

1. There is no scientific evidence to confirm that any alternative, herbal or natural remedies raise the platelet count in the medium to long term. Platelet counts may well increase in some people in the short term. But it is impossible to tell whether or not the increase is really due to the alternative remedy or just general fluctuations in our platelet count due to changes in our overall health etc.

2. No official registers are maintained anywhere to record side effects or results which may be caused by alternative, herbal or natural remedies including Aloe Vera juice and Papaya Leaf extract. With conventional ITP treatments full records are kept and updated with details of any side effects encountered.

3. There hasn't been any research on the true impact of alternative, herbal or natural remedies. The bottom line is that we just don't know.

4. There are many dangers in using these types of remedies. It is virtually impossible for us as potential users to actually test/verify exactly what we are taking. We just can't really tell what is in the remedy. Is it what it says it is ? With so many unscrupulous sellers especially via the Internet, it's impossible to be totally sure what we are taking.

5. There are no sure and certain guidelines as to exactly how much of these remedies we should take. This is unlike conventional treatments where prescription is supervised by our specialists and our responses monitored carefully.

6. Surely if it really was possible to raise our platelet counts and control our ITP by taking a relatively simple herbal, natural or alternative concoction then why wouldn't any of the many ITP specialists I have discussed it with suggest or recommend it ?

7.   None of the many ITP specialists I have discussed such remedies with have had any hope that they would work. Their general reaction has been that sadly it is just wishful thinking or clutching at straws.

8.   The very latest research into ITP and its' causes confirms that there is a whole host of very complicated processes going on in the immune systems of ITP sufferers. It has become increasingly apparent that ITP and the causes of it are far more complex than we have previously thought.

These are the issues that have driven my decision to stick with conventional treatments for my ITP.

Another topic which often raises its' head when discussing alternative ways of treating ITP, is diet/nutrition. There are many suggestions that consuming certain foods or combinations of them will assist the platelet count or possibly cure our illness. Sadly ITP is a much more complex illness than that. Indeed recent findings from a research team at Hammersmith Hospital/Imperial College London suggest that ITP may be not just one disease but a group of pathophysiologically distinct processes resulting in immune mediated thrombocytopenia.

Certainly there is absolutely every reason to eat and drink healthily. By that I mean eating plenty of fresh fruit and vegetables (green vegetables especially like kale, broccoli, spinach), minimising the amount of processed foods, eating red meat in moderation, eating less junk food, drinking more water and less alcohol , not smoking and getting plenty of rest/sleep. It's called common sense.

All these things will assist our overall health and wellbeing, including keeping our immune systems healthy and hopefully platelet production plentiful. Drinking too much alcohol damages the liver which is responsible for production of Thrombopoeitin. This is the substance in our systems which regulates the production of platelets in our bone marrow.

I have made a conscious decision to treat my ITP with conventional medicine. I have decided that there are no miracle cures for ITP. I am not going to risk any nostrum potions and expose my health to quackery. However, I have always had full and frank discussions with my ITP specialists and regularly got second opinions along the way.

My thinking about my illness is driven by the opinions of the specialists. If our ITP riddle could be solved by a cocktail of herbal, natural, nutritional remedies, then surely my specialist would have suggested it by now. The truth is that ITP is very, very complex and because it is so rare we simply haven't done enough research yet to really know with any certainty what such off piste remedies can offer.

The most important thing I will say is........Never take anything at all without discussing it in full with your ITP specialist/doctor. Do get a range of opinions from more than one ITP specialist and remember it is your ITP and you need to ensure you get as much information as possible to make the best treatment decisions for you.

CHAPTER FOURTEEN

What I Want Is Facts

"Now, what I want is Facts. Teach these boys and girls nothing but Facts. Facts alone are wanted in life. Plant nothing else, and root out everything else". (From *Hard Times* - Charles Dickens).

One of the main issues I have had with my purple invader is coming to terms with the indefinite nature of the illness. I'm sure most ITP sufferers will know the feeling. It's when all the questions that you ask about ITP, get answered with another question or a bland non-committal statement. Sometimes it's along the lines of.... Well we just don't know, we haven't really got sufficient evidence etc, etc, etc. The other classic statement is .... Everyone is different, we all get different symptoms to different degrees and we all respond differently to the various treatments, blah, blah, blah !

So one of my conclusions about ITP after all these years on board the good ship purple, is that the only definite thing about the illness, is that nothing is definite. But hold on just a minute, like ITP itself that is not completely true. There are actually some very definite things about ITP, many of them established a long time ago.

So in this chapter I thought that it would be useful to put together a list of some of the things we DO actually know about ITP. Whilst compiling this list, I became increasingly amazed at just how much we have discovered.

Let's start with some of the history of our illness....

1.   After initial reports by Portuguese physician Amato Lusitano in 1556 and Lazarus de la Rivière (physician to the King of France) in 1658, it was the German

physician Paul Gottlieb Werlhof who in 1735 wrote the most complete initial report of the purpura of ITP. Platelets were unknown at the time. The name "Werlhof's disease" was subsequently used for ITP until more recent times.

2.	In the 1880s several investigators linked purpura (bruising) with abnormalities in platelet count. The first report of a successful therapy for ITP was in 1916, when a young Polish medical student, Paul Kaznelson, described a female patient's response to a splenectomy. Splenectomy remained a first-line remedy until the introduction of steroid therapy in the 1950s.

3.	A greater understanding of ITP came as a result of a series of experiments in 1951 by scientists Harrington and Hollingsworth. They confirmed that something in the blood of ITP sufferers was the cause of the low platelet counts being seen in ITP patients.

4.	The name given to ITP was changed from Idiopathic Thrombocytopenic Purpura to Immune Thrombocytopenic Purpura from 1951. More recently it has become known as Immune Thrombocytopenia although it is still most commonly known by the letters ITP.

5.	Corticosteroids were first used to treat ITP in the 1950's and a number of other immune suppressing agents like Azathioprine have been used since the 1960's.

6.	IVIG - Intravenous Immunoglobulin was first used to treat ITP in 1980.

7.	The ITP Support Association was founded in the UK in 1995 by Shirley Watson MBE. It became the first support group for ITP sufferers and their families anywhere in the World.

8.	The Platelet Disorder Support Association was founded by Joan Young in 1998 to support ITP sufferers and their families in the United States.

9.	Following research by Professor Julia Newton in 2009 , fatigue was finally recognised as a symptom of ITP.

10.	The International Consensus Report on the Investigation and Management of ITP was published in 2010.

So what else can we say with any certainty about ITP ?

Well, we are also certain about the symptoms of ITP, albeit we recognise that we don't all suffer from all of them or to the same degree of severity. The main symptoms are as follows...

A) Common symptoms...

Petiechiae (small pinprick rash)
Unexplained bruising
Nosebleeds
Gum bleeds
Black mouth blisters
Fatigue
Heavy periods

B) Rarer symptoms...

Blood in the eyes
Bleeding from the ears
Blood in the urine and/or stools
Bleeding from the gut
Bleeding into the brain or other main organs

Further to all this we know that ITP is an auto Immune illness/condition, where our immune system mistakenly destroys our own platelets leading to a low platelet count. The platelet count in a non ITP sufferer is between 150,000 to 400,000 per micro litre of blood. ITP sufferers sometimes have such a low platelet count that it is often in single thousands of figures. My platelet count was just 4000 when I was diagnosed in 2006.

Diagnosis of ITP can only be done by blood test from which the platelet count can be measured. A bone marrow biopsy (sample) is sometimes taken to confirm the diagnosis of ITP and eliminate the possibility of any other potential causes of the low platelet count. The diagnosis of ITP is completed by process of eliminating all other causes for the platelet count being low and is often referred to as diagnosis by exclusion. Other potential conditions which may cause low platelet counts are... Hepatitis C, HIV, Heliobacter Pylori, Quinine, Anemia, Leukemia, Liver problems. A bone marrow biopsy will confirm whether or not platelet production is normal.

We know that ITP can develop in anyone at any age, and it is not more prevalent in one ethnic or racial group than any another. It is slightly more common in women than men. The illness can develop suddenly in children following certain vaccinations like the MMR jab. Generally in children and younger people ITP clears up as suddenly as it appears (usually within 2 to 6 months). In adults ITP is not as likely to clear up without treatment and often not at all. Sadly there is no cure for ITP although there are numerous treatments.

There is no one single cause for ITP but we are aware that it can be triggered by some things like vaccinations, infections, viruses, even colds, flu, bacteria. It is certainly very difficult to pin down a specific reason why ITP develops in some people rather than others, albeit anyone who develops ITP must have the genetic make up to do so.

Some ITP sufferers find that the reason for their low platelet count is a result of a Heliobacter Pylori infection in the stomach. It is a common bacteria which grows in the digestive tract and attacks the stomach lining. So it is very important for ITP sufferers to get this checked. A blood test will reveal whether or not this is an issue but it is certainly something worth asking your specialist or doctor to look at.

Another cause for low platelet counts in some people is Quinine and this was something that was noticed as long ago as 140 years. Quinine attaches to the surface of our platelets and our antibodies are confused by this masking. Subsequently because of this confusion our antibodies mistakenly attack the platelets hence reducing the platelet count. This is especially relevant for patients who are prescribed Quinine to reduce leg cramps. Incidentally, Quinine is extracted from the bark of the cinchona tree, often referred to as the "fever tree", because of the use of Quinine to treat malaria.

In addition to this, some epilepsy drugs reduce the platelet count. So it is hugely important for ITP sufferers to tell their doctor/specialist about any drugs they have taken at any time for other medical conditions. It is possible that these drugs may be causing lower platelet counts. Similarly it is vital to reveal any previous illnesses or conditions we may have had because some of these illnesses may have or continue to lower the platelet count. The more information we can tell our specialist the better.

Our purple interloper is often confused by non ITP sufferers with Haemophilia. But ITP is absolutely nothing to do with Haemophilia. As an aside, although ITP is actually more prevalent than Haemophilia it is actually less well known. There are many differences between ITP and Haemophilia and the following is a short summary of them :

1. Hæmophilia is inherited and permanent, ITP is not inherited, and can go into remission.

2. Patients suffering from Haemophilia are deficient in one of the 12 factors which act together to form a blood clot. ITP patients are short of platelets which work independently as the initial plug to stop blood leakage, but the rest of the clotting mechanism works normally.

3. In ITP Platelet infusions are only used in emergencies as transfused platelets, like the patient's own platelets, are destroyed by their immune systems very quickly.

So I hope that so far, this chapter has confirmed that we really do know an awful lot about ITP. It may often seem as if we are completely mystified by it but whilst it is clear that ITP is rare and very complex, the truth is that we have made huge progress in understanding the nature of the beast, especially in recent years.

Just to put things into perspective, it is pertinent to remind ourselves that ITP is just one of over 80 auto immune diseases. It is also one of over 6000 rare diseases and literally every day new rare diseases are being discovered. So we have to appreciate that the picture regarding auto immune conditions and rare diseases in general is very much a moveable feast. It's dynamic to say the least and is becoming increasingly complex.

We must acknowledge that because ITP is a very rare condition it is never going to attract the huge amounts of research and funding that the more common illnesses do. But on the positive side, interest in and research into auto immune illnesses as a whole is increasing. In ITP specifically it is heartening to know that we are seeing more interest than ever in researching the illness and uncovering more of its' mysteries.

The interest in research into ITP has really grown, because we as a community are well organised and focused, with very well run support groups like the ITP Support Association in the UK and the Platelet Disorder Support Association in the United States. There are numerous other, well organised support groups across the World too. Remember that the UK and US organisations were only founded in 1995 and 1998 respectively, so the research has gradually followed their lead. Drawing attention to the illness, spreading awareness, organising ourselves into proper respected support groups means we are taken more seriously. Researchers, health professionals and pharmaceutical companies, hopefully, will continue to want to work with us.

As a general overview of what we have recently discovered about ITP, it is fair to say that it is a far more complex illness than we had thought. As previously mentioned recent studies by Hammersmith Hospital/Imperial College London suggest that there is a group of very complicated pathophysiologically distinct processes going on with ITP sufferers, ending up in mediated thrombocytopenia. Trying to understand these processes more will enable ITP specialists to work out which treatments are most appropriate for each individual sufferer, rather than using a scatter gun approach.

In terms of treatment we've traditionally been looking at a standard menu of options then going down the list almost religiously trying each one until something works (or doesn't). We then often try it again hoping for a different outcome. (if you think that sounds like the definition of madness, well actually it is). Clearly we need to change the approach.

For us patients, some of the traditional treatment approaches for ITP have been costly, time consuming, frustrating and even worse, have generated horrible side effects. We have carried on that way for a long time. But research and most importantly patient feedback is now telling us that we can more quickly be more accurate and certain about which treatments are most likely to succeed in individual patients.

We have to remember that it wasn't until the 1950's that we even used anything other than splenectomy to treat ITP. Our much despised steroids were not really used widely until the 1960's. We have subsequently developed plenty of treatment options. The secret now is to use them more efficiently and try to more accurately target individual sufferers with the treatment or combination of treatments that are likely to be most successful for them.

On the subject of treatment combinations, this is an area where research is being carried out to examine the effectiveness of using a mix of drugs to get a faster, longer lived response, in ITP patients. Specifically we all know the horrors of the side effects of Prednisolone. So a research team at Bristol University Hospital in the U.K is looking at using a combination of Prednisolone at much lower dosage and Mycophenolate Mofetil (MMF) at the FIRST stage of treatment to minimise the rotten side effects of the steroid. Similar efforts are being looked at with use of TPO drugs in conjunction with a lower steroid dosage but using them at an early stage.

This research is very important because it allows full records and results to be kept and proper monitoring of the patient rather than treatment being issued on an ad hoc basis. We really need to drill down and focus on the responses to the combinations of treatments so that we know what works best. Until now we really don't know, it's just not been focused enough. So it has tended to be trial and error rather than tailoring specific drugs or combinations of drugs or agents for specific patients. Now I'm not suggesting that in future treatment will be tailored to Saville Row standards but at least it might fit each individual a little better. It hopefully won't continue to be off the peg. We cannot continue with a standard menu of rigid options that everyone has to fit into.

The treatment options themselves have been revolutionised in recent years by the introduction of TPO drugs. These drugs have been specifically developed to target ITP which of course none of the older drugs were. The TPO options have only been available since 2008 but have already made a huge impact, providing very good results so far. It is perhaps important here to explain the differences between the TPO drugs and other, older treatment options.

The TPO drugs are....

1. Eltrombopag (Known as Revolade in the U.K, known as Promacta in the U.S).

2. N-Plate known as Romiplostim

These drugs are designed to stimulate platelet production and therefore attack the problem of ITP in a completely different way to the traditional treatment options. This is a huge leap and completely different from most of the other, older treatments.

Drugs like Prednisolone (and other Corticosteroids), Azathioprine, Mycophenolate Mofetil, Rituximab, Cyclosporine, Danazol, Viniceristin are immune suppressing (they are designed to suppress our immune systems and by doing so they slow down our immune systems' ability to destroy our own platelets).

Other treatments like IVIG (Intravenous Immunoglobulin) and Anti -D block platelet destruction. None of the immune suppressing drugs or platelet destruction blocking options are specifically designed for ITP but are drugs which have been used in ITP treatment over the years. Splenectomy is of course another option but tends to be used very, very rarely now, albeit for some ITP sufferers it can often be a good option especially if all other options have been tried and failed.

The TPO drugs have been a massive leap forward. They have given us a completely new way of looking at treating ITP. They have been very successful so far and have seen the use of splenectomy reduce dramatically. Compared to even when I was declared purple in 2006, we have so many more treatment options. The secret as we move forward is being able to target which treatments are most likely to work, in the most effective way.

In ITP we are seeing Immune system disruption. Research has confirmed that in ITP patients generally, there are too many B Cells in our spleens and it is these B Cells which are likely to be responsible for destroying platelets. We also understand that T Cells can destroy platelets in our Bone Marrow. In ITP patients our T Cells and B Cells are not normal. In fact our T Cell numbers tend to be low. We also know that in ITP we see lots of inflammation in our Cells. What we haven't pinned down YET is why this is the case.

Something that we have accepted is that anything from 30per cent to 50per cent of the cause of ITP is genetic. BUT just because someone has the genetic make up necessary to develop ITP , it doesn't mean that they will actually go on and develop it. So what we are saying is... you have to have the genetic make up in the first place to even possibly develop ITP but you also have to encounter other factors too in order for ITP to develop.

So it is not just genetics. The other factors are likely to be some of or a combination of ....

    1.   Environmental...stress, lifestyle.

    2.   Hormonal...can't just be coincidence that more women than men develop ITP.

    3.   Infection...immune system going off kilter after flu, virus, infection.

4.   Vaccination..immune system response to immunisations like MMR.

5.   Other autoimmune illnesses like Lupus.

6.   Heliobacter Pylori bacteria ... confuses the immune system.

7.   Diet....albeit this is very difficult to prove (see the following link to current research ...http://www.itpsupport.org.uk/foodintolerance.htm

The difficulty is that for each individual ITP sufferer, it is almost impossible to detect which one or combination of the above factors may have triggered their ITP. All ITP sufferers will definitely have the genetic make up to be ITP candidates but it is the X factor issues that provoke us to actually develop the purpleness.

Because of this complexity it is very difficult to develop a one size fits all cure. But current ongoing research and greater focus on recording responses to treatments means that we can start to be more successful in getting better at predicting which treatment is most likely to work best for each individual.

One thing we are sure of is that the number of splenectomies being done has reduced dramatically since the TPO drugs have been made available. We have far more treatment options now for ITP than ever and there is a far greater interest in ITP and research into it than we have ever seen before.

What we can conclude now is that we really do know much more about ITP and the potential causes than we have ever done. But we still have a long way to go. We have more research than ever being done and more treatments available. Sadly though we have to be realistic and acknowledge that recent research has confirmed that ITP is actually much more complex than we may have previously thought. No surprise there then, but every cause to be optimistic that we might continue to make progress in unpicking the purple knots.

CHAPTER FIFTEEN

Surviving The Alamo

As I started out on another ITP year in January 2017 it was hard to believe that another Rare Disease Day was approaching so quickly. The 2017 event was the tenth annual Rare Disease Day. But before getting ready for Rare Disease Day I had an important 3 monthly ITP check up to attend. By way of recap, I had been on Mycophenolate Mofetil (MMF), since April 2016 and I was grateful that so far it had worked for me. I last had a hospital check up in November 2016 when my platelet count was 156. So my presence at hospital had not been required again until February 13th 2017.

My visits to the hospital for check ups are carried out with military precision. After well over a decade of purple I had become quite professional at hospital check ups. It's one of the things I could claim to be pretty much an expert at. I arrive about 1 and a half hours before my actual appointment and I immediately get a blood test done. This then allows for the results to be processed in time for me to discuss the vital numbers and the way forward with my specialist at the appointed time. If you wish to revisit my full hospital check up routine, you may recall that it has already been described in full detail in Chapter Nine.

Quite often there is a queue of people in line at the blood test department/clinic but luckily, purple people get priority and jump the queue even though it does attract a good deal of stink eye from other patients. Well my check up on Monday February 13th 2017 confirmed for me ,that all the problems that have been so widely reported about a crisis in the National Health Service (NHS) here in the UK, were well and truly accurate.

I could not believe how busy the blood test clinic was. It is difficult to comprehend that there are so many sick people. Bearing in mind that Reading, my home town, is hardly anything like as busy as our major Cities like say London, Manchester, Leeds, Liverpool, Glasgow, Birmingham where population numbers are just so much bigger. My mind was well and truly boggled, when at 8am there were already about 100 people in the queue waiting to have a blood test. Literally every seat in the waiting area and in the makeshift overflow area in the corridor was taken. And just as a reminder, this was 8am, yes 8am !!! The clinic had already been open for an hour.

Trying to stem this tide of Berkshire humanity were just 4 amazingly cheerful, professional, phlegmatic phlebotomists. How these wonderful people manage to carry on, carrying on is beyond me. Let's face it, how many of us could keep smiling when faced with over 100 people (some of them agitated, grumpy, even occasionally aggressive) at any time, least of all first thing on a Monday morning ? But these incredible warriors do so, day in and day out.

When I arrived at the clinic and witnessed the sheer numbers of people, my mind conjured up an image of Sir Michael Caine in the film ZULU (the tale of the Battle of Rorke's Drift). I am not usually one for drama or hyperbole but it really felt like I had survived the battle of the Alamo that Monday morning. Having said that I quite liked the Alamo when I visited it and the lovely City of San Antonio Texas some 15 years ago. I recall being the only person in the San Antonio River Walk shopping mall NOT wearing a cowboy hat. Strange the things we remember. Anyway, I digress but if I felt utterly bemused and besieged on my blood clinic visit, imagine what the incredible nurses/ phlebotomists working there must have been feeling.

Having survived the actual blood test, I went for a much needed cup of coffee, but those wonderful nurses couldn't do that, they had a full waiting room of people to process ALL DAY from 7am. I assume they get breaks during the day but even so we need to award these people medals let alone a living wage. I just don't know how they do it ?

Despite the huge numbers of people waiting for a blood test, my result was all processed within an hour and I was seen 30 minutes EARLY by my specialist. Due to be seen at 10:40am, I was beckoned into the inner sanctum of examination room 7 at 10:10am.

Even better news came my way once I actually did see my specialist. My platelet count had increased to 198 so clearly the Mycophenolate Mofetil (MMF) was working. Since starting on MMF my dosage had been 2 times 750 milligrams per day and I was now being reduced to 2 times 500 milligrams per day. The only side effects I seemed to get from the drug were occasional nausea (especially mid morning) and difficulty getting to sleep (shades of Prednisolone). But I really couldn't complain, and I was grateful to be in remission.

So with my platelets behaving impeccably I turned my attention to Rare Disease Day and attending the House of Commons Reception on February 28th. I have been fortunate to attend the annual House of Commons Rare Disease Day Receptions on each of the last 5 years (except 2016 when my platelets were wonky or more accurately invisible).

The whole event is a great way to focus the attention of politicians, researchers, health professionals, support services and rare disease charities. The reception gathers people from so many different strands of the rare disease world. From my point of view it reminds me that we are NOT ALONE, and we do have voices, albeit we need to use them. You see the key thing is that if we don't tell people about our issues, our worries, our concerns, our needs then frankly who else will ? We have to tell people because they WON'T just ask. Only we can be our advocates because only we know what we are going through.

The best thing about the reception is meeting other people with different rare illnesses. There really are some outstanding folk amongst our number, campaigning, working, agitating, arguing our case with great force. Individually we are rare but together we have strength and the considerable weight of numbers. I have personally drawn great confidence from knowing that there are over 3.5 million people in the UK with a rare disease, and over 30 million rare disease sufferers in the United States and the same number in the European Union. None of this gets me more platelets or cures my ITP but it certainly does raise my spirits. I am not that rare after all !

For 2017 the theme for Rare Disease Day was *Research* and we all realise how important that is. In a World where the more well known illnesses understandably attract the most research funding and consequently more researchers willing to get involved, we rarer folk are always going to be battling for a share of the spoils. Not only is it about money though. It is about focus, quality of research and direction. We have to demonstrate that we are credible, organised and that we are here. If we don't make any noise, then nobody will hear us ! Simple really.

I cannot stress how important it is for us all to get involved with Rare Disease Day in some way and I make no apology for repeating what I have said in earlier chapters. It is possible to join in with the Rare Disease Day event in simple, modest ways or if you wish to be more animated there are plenty of avenues to explore. The important thing is to do something.

On our behalf, here in the UK, I cannot emphasise enough just how much Rare Disease UK do . We are fortunate indeed to have such terrific people stepping up to the plate for us. One key example of how they have focused attention on the needs of rare disease sufferers is in the publication of the UK Strategy for Rare Diseases in 2013. This was by no means easy to achieve, bearing in mind that it had to encompass the views of numerous agencies across all 4 health authorities of the UK (England, Scotland, Wales and Northern Ireland).

The key features of the strategy may be viewed at the following link..https://www.raredisease.org.uk/uk-strategy-for-rare-diseases. It is incredible to believe that it took until 2013 for any agreed rare disease strategy to be published but it is all the more impressive because the UK is one of the few countries that actually has one at all.

The key problem since the rare disease strategy was published in 2013 has been getting a plan to implement it. The difficult part has been making progress on the implementation, especially in England. Sigh !!!!

As already mentioned the UK Strategy for Rare Diseases was finally agreed in 2013 and included 51 key commitments. It was agreed that the strategy must be implemented in full across all 4 parts of the UK by 2020. Now that may seem to be ample time but there is a huge amount to do and apparently it involves many complex issues. My own personal view is that 7 years is far too long and the deadline should have been much shorter. It all sounds like the familiar tale of kicking a difficult ball into the long grass.

Let's face it, if you really want to get something done then you will and the stiffer the target or deadline the more urgency you should put into achieving it. I mean 7 years, let's put that into perspective... WW1 lasted just over 4 years, WW2 just short of 6 years and The Beatles entire career as a band lasted only 10 years ! This 7 year implementation really is a hard day's night by comparison me thinks.

England has been much slower than our Welsh, Scottish and Northern Irish counterparts in implementing the Rare Disease strategy. At the Rare Disease Day House of Commons Reception in February 2017 the Minister responsible for rare diseases Nicola Blackwood MP, expressed her determination to make sure that the strategy was implemented by the Department of Health. Without wishing to sound too grumpy..she would say that wouldn't she ? Clearly the implementation of the strategy in England needs sharper focus and more urgency.

A report by the All Party Parliamentary Group on Rare, Genetic and Undiagnosed Conditions, entitled *Leaving No One Behind - Why England Needs An Implementation Plan for the UK Strategy For Rare Diseases* was actually published on Rare Disease Day 2017. The report took 3 months to compile, received evidence from patients, carers, health professionals and experts. It unsurprisingly concluded that the UK Strategy for Rare Diseases has not been implemented in England, and there are a number of commitments where NO ACTION has been taken at all. It does not seem to advise WHY NOT and of course it fails to attach any responsibility. Plus ca change !

So what happens now ? We have a nice, shiny report, expensively put together no doubt. It tells us what we already knew, it confirms that nothing much has been done in England to implement a strategy agreed in 2013 so where do we go from here ? Well as usual the politicians seem to restate that they are committed to delivering the strategy across all of the UK. But they don't seem to say when, how or who by. Actions not words are needed NOW not in some far off realm in another galaxy.

The only thing we can do is continue badgering our MP's (especially in England), to keep rare disease awareness in the faces of those who matter and hold them to account.

But as an ITP sufferer why does it actually matter whether or not we have a UK Strategy for Rare Diseases ? Well, there are many reasons why it is so important for us ITP folk and based on my own experiences, here are just 2 of them….

1. Better diagnosis of rare diseases.
2. Better coordination of care, treatment and follow up

The UK Rare Disease Strategy has 51 key commitments and two of them tackle issues that I soon realised were apparent in my own case. In terms of my own ITP diagnosis it took 7 hours of tests and observation in my local Accident and Emergency (AnE) Unit before a definite diagnosis was issued. The hospital had no ITP specialist on duty on the evening I was at AnE, and had to telephone one to get my diagnosis confirmed.

Please don't think that I am complaining about my diagnosis or the process that was undertaken to get my ITP confirmed. On the contrary, the hospital did everything they could, within their power, to get me diagnosed as soon as possible. But it doesn't mean to say we can't improve things for folk in the future does it ? My story is hardly unique and I am sure other people have even more tales of woe to tell regarding their ITP diagnosis. My story is certainly not likely to be as harrowing as some, I am sure.

Another aspect of my ITP experience which has no doubt been one that other purple people have encountered is the lack of coordination between the various parts of the National Health Service in my treatment. I have had 2 check up appointments booked in for me with my ITP specialist, in both cases I even had letters to confirm the date and time of the appointments. In both instances I checked in at the hospital in good time for the appointments only to be advised that they had unfortunately made a mistake, they had double booked my specialist and had to cancel my appointment. Now again, I am sure that other people have had this or worse but it is just so annoying, taking time off work, the costs involved and the stress of it all too. And don't get me started on hospital parking fees !!

So whilst a UK Rare Disease Strategy will not put everything right at an instant at least it does contain commitments to try to improve things. If we don't push for the strategy to be implemented then nothing will ever change. There are no guarantees that even with a strategy, our lot will radically alter but doing nothing is simply not an option in my view. If you do nothing, I can guarantee that you will get nothing.

What we can all do is join Rare Disease UK for free, because adding to their considerable numbers means the weight of the argument on our behalf grows ever stronger. We owe it to ourselves to press our case. If we don't do it, nobody will. It will get kicked into a field with very long grass.

I am certainly not suggesting that everything is negative because clearly huge strides have been made with the Rare Disease Strategy in the rest of the UK, excluding England. We should indeed be very positive to think that we actually do have a Rare Disease Strategy at all because so many nations do not. But that said, we must get the strategy implemented or it will all have been a waste of time. Of course it is difficult but nothing worthwhile was ever easy !

Further developments have recently been made following a 2019 report published by Rare Disease UK entitled *Illuminating the Rare Reality.* The report highlights that since the 2013 UK Rare Disease Strategy was agreed, significant changes have already taken place and need to be reflected in the strategy. The recommendation from Rare Disease UK to the Government is as follows... Review and refresh the UK Strategy for Rare Diseases before the end of 2020. The strategy has become obsolete as technologies and systems have moved on. Its vision and recommendations urgently need updating to ensure rare disease patients receive high quality services, treatment and support regardless of where they live in the UK.

So as with everything in ITP and rare diseases as a whole, it continues to be dynamic and we have to press hard to get the powers that be to keep pace. My personal worry is that we keep seeing endless reports and they are not in themselves action. I don't think it is unreasonable to suggest that we don't need any more reports, surveys, opinion polls, committees, or any other prevaricating, we just need the original plan to be updated and implemented in full as agreed. As a well known sports brand regularly suggest - 'just do it !'

CHAPTER SIXTEEN

Fatigue and ITP

I have been trying to write this chapter for a few weeks now but I have just been so tired I haven't been able to face it.

This is absolutely NOT true... but how many times have we all heard these sentiments expressed by fellow ITP folk ? If there is one topic which makes us purple people prickly, it is tiredness/fatigue and how it is still not fully recognised as a symptom of our enigmatic illness.

So I thought that it would be a good idea to devote some space here to the subject of fatigue/tiredness. Now stay with me, if you are already nodding off. In this instalment I will look at some of the recent research into the subject. I will also look forward to some new research into tiredness and ITP which is just starting. I will then cover some of the practical things we can all try to combat the effects of fatigue.

A good place to start is reminding myself that the reason I ended up getting diagnosed at all with ITP was that my constant tiredness and general fatigue eventually forced me to visit my doctor. Now as we all know there is tiredness and that is something we can all deal with. But there is also the ITP variety which I call purple chronic fatigue. To anybody without ITP, the sort of fatigue we suffer is almost impossible to explain. It is a completely overwhelming feeling of lethargy, exhaustion, weariness and jadedness. Like a wrung out sponge, a juiceless orange.

With ITP it is clear that you are running on empty and this then gets even worse because the brain doesn't really accept this very readily. I certainly want to just get on with everything at my usual pace and can't comprehend why I am not able to do so. Grumpiness, frustration and generally getting uppity, then takes a hold.

And yet, many ITP sufferers, me included, find that despite all our fatigue experiences and many arguments with numerous ITP specialists and health professionals, fatigue/tiredness is still not generally recognised by many as a symptom of our purpleness.

I recently conducted a poll via the ITP Support Association HealthUnlocked forum about fatigue/tiredness (I am going to abbreviate it to F/T in ITP from now on by the way, as I need to save energy). If you wish to look at the poll, please do so at the following link

....https://healthunlocked.com/itpsupport/polls/135296534/do-you-suffer-from-tiredness-fatigue-and-do-you-think-it-is-linked-to-your-itp.

I was interested to get some feedback on the subject of F/T in ITP. As you will see, the general response was as overwhelming as the tiredness itself. With 104 votes cast, 95 of those people confirmed that YES they did suffer from tiredness/fatigue and they did think it was linked to their ITP. So what ?.... I hear the naysayers and sceptics cry.

The poll in itself is completely unscientific and is just a snap shot for my own interest BUT it does support previous research conducted by a respected ITP expert. Take a look at this next link, if you haven't come across it before....

http://www.ouhsc.edu/platelets/ITP/documents/Newton_et_al-2011-European_Journal_of_Haematology.pdf

It is a terrific piece of research and the most useful part for us purple folk is the concluding paragraph, which I have quoted directly below....

"In conclusion, this study addressed a common complaint of patients with ITP and has objectively quantified the occurrence of fatigue in ITP for the first time, documenting that it is a common symptom that may significantly impact the quality-of-life of patients with ITP. The frequency of fatigue among patients with ITP and its' association with orthostatic symptoms and daytime sleepiness are similar to primary biliary cirrhosis, chronic fatigue syndrome, and other disorders (48), suggesting that interventions that have the potential to improve symptoms of fatigue in these other disorders(26, 48) may also be helpful for patients with ITP. These data provide the basis for future studies to more accurately determine the frequency and severity of fatigue in patients with ITP and define the relation of fatigue to the severity of thrombocytopenia ".

It's not just me then, you don't have to take my word for it, fatigue really is a symptom of ITP and a respected research team have backed up what we have been saying for ages. If you or your ITP specialist or health professional is still not entirely persuaded, what about referring them to another link as follows...

.http://onlinelibrary.wiley.com/store/10.1111/bjh.13385/asset/bjh13385.pdf?v=1&t=j1nppky9&s=26b88d79857a611af7822d86fd484e11077af9ec

Another piece of more recent research into F/T in ITP and again I quote directly from the concluding paragraph as follows....

"Fatigue is an important morbidity from the patient perspective.The presence of fatigue has been established in a significant proportion of patients with ITP. The development of validated, reproducible, disease-specific tools for accessing HRQoL and fatigue has now paved the way for further enquiry into its pathogenesis. Studies of fatigue in chronic disease have found an association between fatigue and symptoms, such as mood and sleep disturbance, and these may be linked through inflammatory processes. The reasons for fatigue are likely to be multiple, vary between individuals and vary for an individual during the course of their illness and treatment. Longitudinal studies are needed to explore the factors contributing to ITP-related fatigue.

Clinicians should assess fatigue symptoms and other aspects of HRQoL alongside lifestyle, bleeding symptoms and the platelet count when considering when to intervene with ITP-directed therapy. The effectiveness of non-pharmacological interventions for fatigue have not been studied in ITP patients but are effective in other chronic disorders, have few adverse effects and may be under- utilised ".

SO.....Fatigue and tiredness is very real, it is now recognised, and acknowledged. It is vitally important to consider it when ITP sufferers are being diagnosed and in giving treatments. The whole area of what is really causing this fatigue and how it is connected to our misfiring immune systems, is now the focus for future research, like that at St James University Hospital in Leeds, where Dr Quentin Hill says...

"We know that up to a third of patients with ITP suffer from significant fatigue but the reason for this is poorly understood ". So the aim of the study is to find out whether changes in the immune system going on in ITP are important in causing fatigue.

Now to us ITP sufferers we would suggest that far more than a third of us suffer from fatigue and it is causing us real problems. So hopefully this new project will provide some real scientific data to back up the anecdotal evidence we have been feeding back for ages. The research team will be looking at how fatigue is influenced by the activity of T and B lymphocytes which are the cells of the immune system involved in the removal of platelets from our circulation. They will also look at a sub-type of lymphocyte called the natural killer (NK) cell. The NK cells can attack virally infected or cancerous cells but also have a role in regulating the immune system. NK cell abnormalities have been found in autoimmune disorders including ITP.

For us ITP sufferers this is all very exciting and even if we cannot fully understand some of the terminology the researchers use, it is just encouraging to know that we are not being ignored. There is a real, genuine interest in getting answers and explanations to what is actually going on with the many processes taking part in our immune systems. It is complicated but like the layers of an onion, the mysteries are slowly being peeled back.

At least we have two very credible pieces of recent research and one important project now getting underway, to share with anyone who questions that tiredness and fatigue really are a symptom of our purpleness. If you are being doubted, show them the articles I have quoted. I can't see how they can ignore them.

So now that fatigue and tiredness have been acknowledged as ITP symptoms, how can we combat the effects of them ? What are some of the other causes of fatigue/tiredness and how we can help ourselves ?

As we purple people know the sort of fatigue we are talking about is not just feeling a bit out of sorts. I can remember times before I was actually diagnosed with ITP when I simply couldn't function. The sort of tiredness we are talking about is irresistible. Once the torpor gets its' claws into you, it is almost impossible to repel. Many times I felt the slow nodding and drooping of my head and then my leaden eyes would have to close. It was impossible to resist. It was like trying to cross the Atlantic Ocean in a shopping trolley from the supermarket. Utterly futile.

So what is fatigue and is it solely a purple problem ? Well it is absolutely not just an ITP issue. Fatigue is one of the most common reasons why people visit their doctor. As I have already mentioned it is the reason that I ended up going to my doctor to get checked out back in July 2006. I had simply had enough of feeling tired all the time.

Extreme tiredness that is present most or all of the time is usually referred to as fatigue. It is recognised as a symptom of many conditions such as heart disease, ME (chronic fatigue syndrome), coeliac disease, iron deficient anaemia, diabetes, cancer, depression, glandular fever and many other illnesses.

Fatigue can of course also be caused or exacerbated by many treatments such as radiotherapy, chemotherapy, antihistamines, steroids and statins. We ITP folk know how badly some of us respond to Prednisolone with many sleepless nights adding to our already exhausted days.

As a further example of drug induced fatigue, many hay fever sufferers become completely unfit for purpose after taking antihistamines. Some of my closest friends and family members literally sink into a stupor during the Spring/Summer. With pollution levels so bad these days in our cities it won't be getting any better any time soon. My home City of London is one of the worst on the planet incidentally.

Fatigue is present in many autoimmune conditions including ITP but it is less well acknowledged and recognised because there is no physical evidence to explain it and no simple way to measure it. We all know too that excessive anxiety, stress, and family problems can be triggers for fatigue. So what can we do about it ?

There are quite a few things that we can do to help combat fatigue. Now I am not suggesting that all of the following things will mean that you enjoy a completely fatigue free life if you do them. Far from it because so many things will work well for one person and not especially well for others. But most of the following suggestions are quite simple, practical things we can all try. Common sense is really the best way of describing these things, so here are a few thoughts, suggestions and ideas. I do however, precede this section with the following important statement -

As ever, it is important to discuss your own individual medical situation with your specialist first before making any changes to your routines/diet/exercise etc.

SLEEP

1.   Go to bed and get up at a regular time if you possibly can. Try to follow the same sleep routine every night.

2.   Try some mental and physical exercise during the day (pretty obvious but worth pointing out), especially late afternoon or early evening and it will help you to sleep.

3.   Only take a short afternoon nap/siesta if it doesn't interfere with your sleep at night.

4. Avoid dozing in front of the TV during the evening by doing other light activities or hobbies like reading, listening to music, having a conversation, writing. Avoid watching too much TV or working on a computer, lap top, tablet, or mobile phone.

5. Keep your bedroom dark (seems obvious but always close the curtains or blinds).

6. Make sure noises in the house during the night are kept to a minimum. So switch off any electrical appliances that are likely to hum, buzz or disturb you.

7. Make sure your bedroom is not too hot.

8. Have a warm, milky drink before you go to bed. BUT avoid anything with caffeine in it. Don't eat anything for a couple of hours before you go to bed and avoid too much alcohol.

9. Try to keep calm if you really cannot sleep.

10. If you are going to be awake look at it as a positive. When I was on Prednisolone and it was keeping me awake I decided that if I was not going to sleep I might as well do something constructive. So I did my Humanities degree with the Open University. It did not help me sleep but I enjoyed spending some of the wee small hours doing something useful.

EATING HEALTHILY

1. Eat a good, fresh, well balanced diet as it gives your body the best chance to fight fatigue. It also helps your body in so many other ways too.

2. In a balanced diet, it is important to eat a healthy mix of protein, carbohydrates, fresh fruit and vegetables. We are all different and may have a variety of other medical issues to consider in addition to our ITP. So it is important to discuss your diet and any changes you might make with your doctor or specialist.

3. With ITP we must avoid quinine and any products that contain quinine. We also need to avoid aspirin, ibuprofen and any products that contain them.

4. Generally eat less salt, lower fat and reduce sugar intakes. If eating ready made meals check very carefully the levels of salt, fats and sugars included as they can be surprisingly high.

5.   Drink plenty of water. This is absolutely vital as dehydration is a major cause of many health problems including kidney stones, kidney infections, urinary tract infections. Dehydration will make you feel lethargic, tired, fatigued and listless.The suggested intake of water per day is 1.2 litres which is somewhere between 6 and 8 glasses(depending on how big your glass is). During hot weather we should drink more.

6.   Avoid too much caffeine. Remember that caffeine is in many drinks, not just coffee & tea. It is in cola, and many soft drinks. Caffeine keeps you awake and also prompts you to urinate more so dehydrating the system. It is also a stimulant and increases the heart rate amongst other things.

7.   Being overweight increases fatigue and tiredness and has many other health risks like the possibility of developing heart disease and cancer. So avoid snacking and too much sugar. Cut down on fats and processed food like ready meals and take away foods such as burgers, pizza, fried chicken. You can still eat these things but they really should only be an occasional "treat" option. Eat more fresh fruit and vegetables .

8.   Cook your own meals. This sounds a bit trite but it really is important. In cooking and preparing your own food YOU know what is going into it. YOU can control the amount of fats, sugars, salts that you are eating by measuring how much of it you are putting in your food.

9.   Greens Greens Greens....For us ITP folk, green vegetables and fruits are essential. Consuming spinach, kale, cabbage, lettuce, broccoli, apples and pears is very helpful in boosting the health of our immune system. Greens contain plenty of Vitamins A, C, E, and K. (they help in the clotting process).

REDUCING STRESS

1.   In the modern world, it is virtually impossible to eliminate all stress from our lives. That said, we do actually need a certain amount of stress to function properly. BUT it is being able to control, manage and limit the stress levels that really sorts out how well we live and how healthy we are.

2.   Try to include some relaxation in your day to day existence. So making sure you go out and have a walk every day is a really good way to do this. Getting some fresh air is so beneficial, it not only clears the mind but it helps our physical well being. It helps the joints and muscles, and has many other benefits.

3. Take some time every day for you. Listen to some music, read, have a warm bath, smile, talk to family and friends, watch something funny, go to the movies, take up a hobby, go to a museum, visit a gallery. Go do something !

4. Turn off your phones, computers, iPads, gadgets, tablets. Have some down time. Be unavailable for at least a while every day. Nothing is more important than your peace of mind and long term health. The World can wait occasionally. None of us are indispensable or irreplaceable.

5. Pace yourself, be realistic about goals you set.

6. Maintain contact with your family and friends and share your feelings with them. Fatigue and stress are not visible to other people, so talk to someone about what you are going through. Remember you can also use the many ITP social media forums/support groups and share your experiences with other like suffering folk.

7. Avoid stressful situations. It sounds ridiculous but sometimes the smallest word is one that is the most difficult to use. The word I am thinking of is no. Sometimes for your own good say no.

8. Along with saying no, keep a detailed planner/diary system. Make sure people around you know what that planner consists of. Don't allow people to double book you or steal your time. Be clear what you want and when you are available to do it. You have to manage it or it will manage you. It might even kill you !

9. Plan properly. The old adage of "failing to plan and planning to fail" is one of the truest of them all. So plan well and know what success actually is, know what you are actually aiming to do, when you are aiming to do it by, how you are going to do it, who is going to help you achieve it and know when you have achieved it.

10. Don't be afraid to ask for help. It sounds simple doesn't it but so many people take everything on themselves and forget that a problem aired is a problem shared.

11. Tell your doctor , ITP specialist, consultant if you are feeling stressed, fatigued, tired. You would tell them if you have a nosebleed or bruise so tell them about stress, fatigue and tiredness.

12. Join in with local group meetings and social media forums. The ITP Support Association and the Platelet Support Disorder Association amongst others have regular local and national meetings and forums on Facebook, Twitter and there is also the ITP Support Association HealthUnlocked group.

13.   Get a little bit of sun. Not getting enough sunlight can exacerbate fatigue and feelings of tiredness. Obviously too much sun has other negative effects like causing skin and other cancers but a little exposure to the sun (sensibly before 10am) is useful. A walk in the early morning sun or evening at the seaside or in the country is one of life's real treats and has so many beneficial aspects. But always wear a hat, drink plenty of water and wear a high factor sun lotion.

EXERCISE

1.   Many medical and scientific studies confirm that exercise really does boost energy levels. It improves the efficiency of your heart, circulatory system, lungs and muscles and is good for the brain. It also aids flexibility and helps prevent obesity and all the negative health issues that may arise from it.

2.   You don't need to do too much. Be sensible, start slowly and discuss any plans you have to start exercising with your doctor or specialist first

3.   Regular light exercise is proven to be beneficial to combating fatigue. Just a short walk every day is a great start.

4.   Cycling and swimming are great alternatives to just walking or jogging.

5.   Don't sit too long. Even if you move around in the garden cutting the grass, picking up leaves, just pottering around, it is all helpful.

6.   Just getting some fresh air will help to relieve stress, improve your sleep and reduce tiredness.

Most of these suggestions are really common sense and probably things that we all think that we are already doing. But if we are honest, we probably don't do them anywhere near enough. I call them my should do's but don't always do's. That said, the most important thing with all of it is that it should not become too onerous because if it is then you will never stick to it. You have to make it fun, simple and really want to do it.

One thing that is never fun is visiting the hospital but my own ITP journey continued with yet another blood test on April 5th 2017. My last meeting with my specialist had taken place on February 13th and the welcome news was that my platelet count was a very satisfactory 198. My specialist wanted to see me again on May 15th but have an interim blood test on April 5th, just to keep an eye on things midway between appointments. I had been on Mycophenolate Mofetil (MMF) since April 2016 and my counts had been well over 100 since June (the MMF took 3 months to impact fully on the platelet count, which is quite normal).

I had become mildly comfortable with my ITP. This comfort is not the sort of cosy you get when wearing your favourite sneakers (training shoes) but the sort of comfortable you get when you suddenly realise that you are not completely lost. You suddenly recognise somewhere as being acceptably familiar. I suppose it is a restless, ease, if that makes sense. I have learned how to live with it and it has learned how to put up with me.

Anyway, back to my blood test on April 5th. I arrived at the blood test clinic at the crazy hour of 06:45 thinking that I would steal a march on most of the early birds trying to catch their worms. The clinic opens at 07:00 so I thought that I would be one of the few people to arrive before the opening hour. Wrong ! I was only number 9 in the queue. Incredibly number 1 had started his vigil at 06 : 00.

As ever in Britain, we each took our place in the queue resignedly and waited our respective fates. We may be slightly eccentric but the one thing we do really well in Britain is queue. If the Olympic Games included it as an event we would undoubtedly go, in orderly fashion, to the front of the line for a Gold medal.

The blood test result was absolutely solid when I telephoned my specialist a couple of days later. He said that my count was still over 150 and that I should see him again, as previously planned on May 15th. So no further requirement apart from to carry on with the MMF at a dosage of 500 mg, twice a day.

One very helpful extra piece of advice I received during my discussions with the phlebotomist concerned clumping platelets. Now, I had a couple of incidents of this very thing back in January and February 2015, so I have got history. Platelets are more likely to clump if you are dehydrated, so yet another very good reason to drink plenty of water. In my case the clumping I experienced was actually due to the blood sample being processed incorrectly but even so the need to H2O is well noted. I'll certainly be raising a glass or two, or maybe even eight a day to that from now on ! Cheers !

CHAPTER SEVENTEEN

Age Concern ?

Like many other purple people, I still find myself asking numerous questions about this irritating illness. The problem I found on diagnosis was that I had so many questions that it was a bit like trying to be a plate spinner with your hands in your pockets. I knew what I wanted to know but couldn't get the questions out and in the correct order. Even when I did get the questions right I couldn't really process the answers logically. I am the sort of person who likes to really understand things. Once I know something I can deal with it, albeit ITP is quite difficult to process in simple, logical terms. Our wretched illness is illogical, there are very few clearcut answers. It's not the ideal disease for someone as pedantic as me.

One of the key questions of course was - why me ? How have I developed ITP when I have had a previously completely healthy life ? The answer of course is that truthfully we don't really know for sure. It could be a combination of many factors . But we do know that to develop ITP you have to be genetically predisposed to do so. However, even if you have got the right (or should it be wrong) genetic make up, it does not mean that you will definitely develop ITP. There have to be other triggers and these can be many and varied. I will set out my own thoughts on this in the final chapter of this book.

For the purposes of this chapter, a couple of age related questions that I have repeatedly asked since my diagnosis are…Has ITP got anything to do with age ? Does ITP develop in certain age groups more than others? The simple one word answers I kept getting for both questions was no. But is there any age concern ? What has age got to do with it ? What do we need to know about age and ITP ?

Well here goes………

We know that you can develop ITP at any age. It can occur in very young children, in teenagers, young adults, folk like me of middle age, and equally in people who are more senior. ITP does not discriminate BUT I have always been eager to know whether ITP is more prevalent in one age group or groups than another ? So to help me I set a poll on the ITP Support Association HealthUnlocked forum. The question I asked was a very simple one...

....At what age were you diagnosed with ITP ?

https://healthunlocked.com/itpsupport/polls/135375685/at-what-age-were-you-diagnosed-with-itp-please-use-the-age-of-any-child-you-are-answering-this-poll-on-behalf-of

Whilst the poll is clearly random, completely unscientific and uncontrolled it did broadly support other evidence about the incidence of ITP in certain age groups. The poll received 134 responses and 63 people (i.e. about 47 per cent) were diagnosed between the ages of 20 and 50 which actually reinforces more respected findings. See the following link :

http://emedicine.medscape.com/article/779545-overview#a7)

Obviously what would be nice to know as a follow up, are the factors which might have caused diagnosis of these people at that stage in their lives. For example it could well be that a good number of these folk developed ITP during or straight after pregnancy. But possibly that is a question for another survey. What we do know is that the ratio between male and female cases tends to widen with age, with more female cases than male. For example in the USA the chronic, adult ITP population records women outnumbering men by 2 to 1.

The next piece of information I found suggests that adult ITP is more likely to be chronic and there is somewhere between a 20 per cent and 40 per cent possibility of a lasting remission from it in adults. See the following link :

https://en.wikipedia.org/wiki/Immune_thrombocytopenic_purpura

The age analysis in younger people with ITP confirms that about 40 to 50 percent of all new ITP cases diagnosed each year are children. Around 40 percent of cases are children between the ages of 2 and 4. Now these figures are not borne out by our own random study and there is a very logical reason why. Children in that age range cannot use the internet so cannot respond to a survey on a HealthUnlocked forum, so we are dependent on a parent or guardian to answer for them . Realistically responses in this group are likely to be fewer.

The very good news with ITP in children is that about 70 percent of cases will go into remission within 6 months of diagnosis, many without any treatment at all. Hence there is a reluctance to treat children with any drugs unless symptoms are severe or threatening or other medical issues are involved.

So from just a little bit of my own research I have concluded the following things about ITP and age...

1. The most popular age range that people get diagnosed with ITP is between 20 and 50. I am living, breathing proof that this is the case. I was diagnosed at the age of 46.

2. The chances of being diagnosed with CHRONIC ITP are higher as you get older. In children ITP tends to be of the ACCUTE type (i.e. it goes away almost as suddenly as it appears and usually within 3 to 6 months).

3. More women than men are diagnosed with ITP, with the ratio increasing to about 2 to 1 in adults with chronic ITP

4. Around 40 percent of children diagnosed with ITP are between ages 2 to 4 and about 50 percent of all new ITP cases diagnosed each year are children.

5. About 70 to 80 percent of children diagnosed with ITP go into remission within 6 months (https://itpsupport.org.uk/index.php/en/the-childhood-itp-registry).

6. ITP is a condition that you can be diagnosed with at any age.

7. Young platelets are more effective than old ones. What does that mean I hear you scream ? OK I will hopefully explain or at least relay what I understand about the subject as it was explained by Dr Jecko Thachill of the Manchester Royal Infirmary, who is also a member of the ITP Support Association Medical Panel (https://itpsupport.org.uk/index.php/en/medical-advisors)

YOUNG PLATELETS versus OLD PLATELETS

All of us purple people know that ITP is a condition where, even though our platelet production is increased from our bone marrow, our misguided immune system destroys platelets even more rapidly hence leading to thrombocytopenia and the tell tale symptoms we all recognise.

Right so far are you with me ? OK.... well we have also discovered that in general, we folk with ITP do not have the same bleeding tendency as those with the same degree of thrombocytopenia caused by a bone marrow issue/problem. So we purple folk in general don't tend to bleed as much as those with bone marrow/platelet production issues. Our problem is one of destruction rather than production (in general terms). Also the platelet count in us purple people is actually a poor predictor of whether or not we are actually likely to suffer any bleeding be it internal (brain bleeds or internal organs) or external (nose bleeds, gum bleeds etc).

So what does all this mean ? In a nutshell in ITP because we are having to produce so many more platelets because our misfiring immune systems keeps destroying them it means a much higher proportion of our platelets are young. Well so what, one might say ? Well so good actually. Younger platelets are more capable of stopping bleeding than older ones and this may explain the general tendency for less bleeding in ITP patients than those with platelet production/bone marrow deficiencies.

So in platelets the younger the better and so platelet age really is a definite factor. But it's not just about age, it's also a size issue too. Platelets decrease in size as they get older so the younger platelets are bigger and are therefore more effective in the clotting process.

Now there is a test which can be done to measure the average size of our platelets called the Mean Platelet Volume (MPV). It takes into account the different sizes of platelet circulating in our blood. So if the younger platelets are more predominant our MPV will be greater but if the number of younger platelets is fewer our MPV will be lower. It is as if the ITP Gods have granted us a back handed bonus, a compensatory gift of younger, bigger more efficient platelets in exchange for mistakenly destroying them. One heck of a quid pro quo !

In ITP sufferers our MPV is normally higher than average (again I use the words normally higher with caution) . Now this measure should not be looked at in isolation and cannot be relied upon in itself but it can be viewed at in combination with other evidence/symptoms that the patient is showing.

Just to get a bit more complicated here is another set of initials to get thinking about in respect of the age of our platelets.... IPF which stands for Immature Platelet Fraction. This looks at the number of young platelets circulating in our blood system and it can give an indication of whether or not there is a likelihood that even with a low platelet count there is likely to be bleeding or not.

With IPF and MPV all this is just another aspect of estimating/predicting whether or not the patient is at risk from bleeding or at least getting a better idea of the bleeding propensity.

So what can we conclude about the age of our platelets ?

1.   In general young platelets are more plentiful in ITP sufferers because we produce more of them to replace those being destroyed by our misfiring immune systems.

2.   Young platelets tend to be bigger and therefore are more efficient in the clotting process.

3.   Testing can be done in the lab to check the volume of younger platelets and age of them in our systems. Hence it gives more information to our specialists when they consider whether or not we each have a greater or lesser propensity to bleed even with lower platelet counts.

4.   This is an area still developing all the time and we are getting more ammunition to be able to design treatments specifically for patients as individuals.

5.   Age and size really does matter with platelets.

Hopefully this chapter has covered a lot of age concerns both in terms of what age has got to do with being diagnosed purple and what relevance is the age of our platelets. I have certainly concluded that age does not discriminate when it comes to ITP.

We know that anyone at any age can develop ITP and they can do so for a wide range of reasons. In children ITP tends to be more likely to go into remission than adults and in us grown ups we are more likely to be chronic.

As we are discovering more about our illness we are certainly better able to tailor treatments to the individual sufferer with more precision and I am a firm believer that sharing our individual stories plays a big part in helping this process. I have added a list of sources at the end of this book which is by no means extensive. It is a list of the wide variety of purple people of all ages who have been courageous and creative enough to write up their stories in blog, book or website form. There are many others but I simply didn't have the space to include them all.

CHAPTER EIGHTEEN

If I Knew Back Then, What I Know Now

One abiding memory I have of the day that I was originally told that I had ITP is wondering where I could get any information about it. I couldn't even pronounce the name of the disease properly. I could barely understand what the doctors and nurses were telling me and I simply could not digest the explanations being provided.

In this chapter I will look at the most useful sources of information I have discovered in my ITP years. I am sure that I will cover many of the most popular ones but the list is by no means exhaustive. Many ITP sufferers will have other useful sources and if I have omitted any it is because I have not personally found them yet. I will conclude the chapter by revealing the top ten lessons that I have learned during my purple experience. If only I'd have known then what I know now !

The problem I found on my diagnosis was that I had so many questions. I am sure that all ITP sufferers will have felt exactly the same as I did then. It took me ages to get my head around the idea that my illness was even remotely serious. I didn't feel particularly unwell and apart from being quite tired and having a few random bruises, I didn't look ill. In fact, I only really started feeling unwell once I commenced the Prednisolone treatment.

Looking back to that time, I can safely say that for me it was certainly more a matter of mental anguish than any physical pain or feeling ill. It is the uncertainty of not really understanding what is actually wrong with you that gets the mind ticking. So many unanswered questions (in all honesty, at least for the first 6 months, nearly all unanswered questions), so much information to deal with, numerous appointments to attend. For ages I felt like a kite in a hurricane.

So where can a purple person turn to for help ? Well back in 2006 the entire ITP climate was vastly different to the relatively balmy weather we've got nowadays. I know that this may seem like I'm coming across as a grumpy old, purple timer. But the truth is that information about ITP is now just so much more readily available. Undoubtedly the ability to Google just about everything has made a huge difference. To put things into context, Facebook was only set up in 2004 and Twitter appeared in 2006. Even the World Wide Web had only been around for 10 years. The information landscape was very different. I'm sure dinosaurs still roamed around freely searching for Alexa and Siri !

A major issue we have now of course, is that we have too much information and it is difficult to know what is useful, accurate, up to date and so what can be trusted. That said, our knowledge of all things ITP has improved exponentially. But with the advent of social media, there is just so much information. Sifting through it and deciding what is really important is now almost a full time job. Facts, information, alternative truths, fake news and all that jazz are now almost inseparable so we need to be even more discerning than ever.

Thankfully for ITP sufferers, the number of treatments, researchers, support groups, blogs, social media forums and general awareness have all made impressive strides. That said, we really must not be complacent because I still come across plenty of people, even healthcare professionals who have never heard of ITP. It reinforces the need for us all to keep talking about ITP and I am encouraged to persist with this book for that very reason.

Unless we talk about it, then ITP will not get on the agenda anywhere. It is rare and let's be realistic there are other illnesses that will always get more attention. But talking about it and especially, engaging with non purple people, is vital.

Organising ourselves and sharing our experiences would not have been possible without the platforms to air these views on. So the starting point for my useful sources of ITP information has to be the ITP Support Association here in the UK and the Platelet Disorder

Support Association in the United States. Without those two organisations, then frankly I would not be writing this story. I may never have really understood very much about ITP without them and I am sure that we would not have made anything like the progress we have done with treatments, awareness, and understanding. They are the foundations on which the ITP house of knowledge has been built.

The ITP Support Association (ITPSA) was established in 1995 by Shirley Watson MBE and was the first support group for ITP sufferers and their families, anywhere in the World. Shirley set up the group because her son had been diagnosed with ITP. At the time, there was scant support, very little information and certainly nowhere to share her worries, concerns and fears. As a parent of a young boy with a very strange, rare condition it must have been frightening enough but realising that there was no support of any kind, must have been even more daunting.

The ITPSA is a UK registered charity, receiving no support or funding from central Government. It is run almost entirely by volunteers and relies on the generosity of members, supporters, friends and families of sufferers. For the first 20 years of its' life the ITPSA was run from a spare outbuilding in Shirley Watson's home. It was only in 2015 that a permanent HQ was built (literally by Shirley and her husband Frank & an army of volunteers), from where the operation continues to grow. The ITP Support Association certainly paved the way for other ITP support groups to follow.

Many readers of this blog will know that from 2010 to December 2017 I worked on a voluntary basis for the ITPSA. I wrote a column for their quarterly publication The Platelet and continue to make written contributions. I also continue to take part in the various social media groups. I am delighted to have been able to help them by setting up and managing their social media platforms. I have been pleased to assist because I see it as an opportunity to share my own ITP experiences and learn from the stories of others. It's also very pleasing to think that I might have made some small contribution towards getting some better answers to our purple riddle.

The ITPSA are available on Facebook, Twitter, HealthUnlocked, Instagram, and LinkedIn. The various platforms are very active and I am sure that many people reading this will have seen or contributed to some of them at some time. If you haven't seen them or joined in, then please do via the following link :

http://www.itpsupport.org.uk/index.php/en/

The information you will find on the main ITPSA website is vetted by a panel of medical advisors, consisting of some of the leading ITP experts in the World. This is a hugely important factor because with so much information available these days, on no end of internet sites, we need to be sure that what we are reading is correct. It is a problem of our times.... we have more information but can we trust it and how can we use it ?

Across the Atlantic, The Platelet Disorder Support Association (PDSA) in the United States was formed in 1998 by Joan Young. As an ITP sufferer since 1992, Joan worked tirelessly to establish a support group in the USA and has seen it go from strength to strength.

The PDSA have numerous support groups across the United States and Canada which can be located at the following link :

https://pdsa.org/join-the-community/local-groups.html .

A brief history of the PDSA is available at : https://pdsa.org/about-us.html .

Both the PDSA and the ITPSA have been instrumental in setting up Global ITP - The ITP International Alliance website which provides full details of the many ITP Support Groups across the World. The website is available at the following link :

http://www.globalitp.org/index.php.

It is a great example of the benefits which we have all derived from cooperation and the sharing of knowledge, information and experiences.

The growing list of ITP Support Groups across the globe is a testament to the amazing work of the many volunteers who have worked so hard to spread purple awareness. There are so many ITP heroes going about their work, mostly on a voluntary basis, and I tip my hat to all of them. I was fortunate enough to meet some of our global purple colleagues at the ITPSA Annual Convention in September 2016 held here in the UK. They are passionate, purple people indeed who do incredible work for our cause.

Since the advent of social media we have seen an explosion of ITP support groups on platforms like Facebook, Twitter, Instagram and others besides. As previously stated the ITP Support Association and the Platelet Disorder Support Association have very active, informative forums on these outlets but there are a number of other ITP related platforms which are interesting, helpful and very supportive. I would suggest that the following may be worth looking at on Facebook...ITP - Spreading Awareness, ITP for Aussies, ITP - In Pregnancy, ITP and Me. There are many others but like anything it is all a matter of personal choice.

All of the groups that I have mentioned are those which I have had contact with myself. The list is not a complete one and in no way should any information or details they mention ever be taken as medical advice. It is always worth reiterating that any information or comments from such sources should never be taken as anything other than to supplement the advice of our ITP specialist or medical professionals. Never do or take anything without discussing it in full with your ITP specialist or doctor beforehand.

Everything in life is always easy with hindsight and having ploughed my own purple ITP furrow, I can certainly reflect now on many aspects of my journey which I would have changed. There are so many things that I would do differently now if I was setting sail on the good ship ITP. So moving forward in this chapter I want to focus on the many lessons I have learned along my ITP road. If just one other ITP sufferer or future purple patient can benefit from any of my good, bad or ugly experiences then I will be content.

LESSON ONE - KNOW THE KEY SYMPTOMS & GET CHECKED OUT

The best place to start with my ITP lessons is unquestionably at the very beginning of my purple journey. In fact, I suppose if you wanted to be pedantic that first lesson is actually before my purple journey began.

Let me explain that a bit. Like many ITP sufferers I had been showing a number of ITP symptoms for about a year before I was ever diagnosed. As mentioned previously (see Chapters 1 and 2), I ignored the warning signs that I had been getting for about a year, before I even went to my doctor to be checked.

If I had my ITP time again the first thing I would do is visit my doctor or hospital as soon as I got any of those symptoms. It would have meant being diagnosed a year earlier. I could have started treatment that much sooner and I would not have seen my platelet count fall to life threateningly low levels of just 4. Ultimately, it could have been worse for me. With such a low platelet count, let's be frank, I could have died.

So lesson one for anyone reading this is please familiarise yourself with the key symptoms of ITP and if you develop any of them get checked out as soon as possible. Do not delay, do not pretend the symptoms could be something insignificant or accidental like I did. The sooner you get checked the better. If in any doubt, get checked out.

LESSON TWO - ALWAYS LOOK on the BRIGHT SIDE of LIFE

This may not seem a very sensible thing to say when discussing ITP, because let's be honest it is not a trivial illness or something to smile about. But it is very important to put ITP into some perspective. It is easy for me to say that after nearly thirteen years living with the purple enigma but if I were starting out on my ITP odyssey today, I would try to worry much less about it.

Yes we know that ITP has no cure and of course it can be very serious in some cases. I would never trivialise the nature of the illness for one minute, I've had some horrible times with it but it is worth trying to keep things in perspective as far as possible. I know this because I didn't do that myself for quite a long time.What gave me that much needed sense of perspective was learning more about our tricky purple condition and also a stark discussion or two with people suffering from things that were very much worse.

Everything fell into place for me when I had my Rituximab treatment in 2010. My own situation was put into sharper focus by discussions with a number of other patients who were definitely suffering far greater than I was. Now, if I explain that ITP patients are treated at the Royal Berkshire Hospital Cancer Centre in my home town, you will probably be able to understand what I am trying to convey here. Whilst ITP is a difficult, cussed condition it can be controlled in most cases. It is not progressive and certainly it is nowhere near as serious as many other illnesses.

Looking back, what I would hope to have done sooner is to realise that ITP is not as serious as many other conditions. It can be controlled and in most cases it is not life threatening as long as it is diagnosed quickly and treated where necessary. I wish that I could have accepted that quicker. There are many, many other things which are much worse. Take some consolation from this, be positive and do not let it stop your life.

LESSON THREE - BE MORE AWARE and KNOW WHERE to LOOK

One of the difficulties of suffering from ITP and any other rare illness for that matter is knowing what the symptoms are, finding out what the illness actually is and trying to understand what is happening in your own body. The key thing is knowledge, information and knowing where to get it. When I was diagnosed the breadth of knowledge about ITP was considerably narrower than it is now. But for me, it was even knowing where to look for information that was a challenge in itself. Even pronouncing or spelling the illness Immune Thrombocytopenia correctly, was a major obstacle.

Having a few reliable sources of information has been invaluable and without doubt if I were diagnosed today the places I would look to straight away for reliable ITP information would be The ITP Support Association in the UK and The Platelet Disorder Support Association in the United States of America.

As mentioned earlier, both organisations are available on the internet and social media, so do look them up. Joining the ITP Support Association here in the UK was certainly one of the most important steps I made with my ITP. It not only gave me access to a phenomenal amount of information but it put me in touch with other ITP sufferers going through so many of the very same things that I was experiencing. Not quite safety in numbers but certainly some comfort.

LESSON FOUR - IT's YOUR ITP so YOU HAVE TO OWN IT

A key thing that I found difficult about my ITP was actually accepting it. By that I mean that it seemed to take me a good while to get beyond denying that I had it. For ages I was constantly shaking my head in disbelief, feeling quite sorry for myself and generally trying to deny the purple. Once I had learned to embrace it, I could better plan to deal with it. So it is very important to realise sooner rather than later that once you have been diagnosed it is better to accept it, and take ownership of the illness.

I found that it is really important to me, to keep full records of my many meetings with doctors and specialists. I have always maintained my own records of appointments, platelet counts, drugs prescribed, dosages of each drug and when I started or stopped any treatment. These days things are made a bit easier for us as there are numerous tools on computer/lap top/cell phone which assist record keeping.

For example, a new ITP Platelet Tracker APP is available now, developed by Novartis and the ITP Support Association. The APP will harness all of the records you would wish to have about your own ITP journey. From the very outset I recorded everything about my ITP in my diaries and subsequently in my blog and now here. I'm not a technophobe and am happy to use technology where I can see that it adds value but I do like pen and paper. I believe that writing something down focuses the mind.

Another aspect of taking ownership of my ITP is making sure that I always ask questions about my treatments and the various options at meetings with my specialists. I always have a number of queries written down in a notepad before appointments. I do a bit of research and some homework before any meetings because the more they can be a two way discussion, the more we both can get out of them. My specialists need my participation as much as I need theirs. They can better help me, if I can better help them, to do so. I also make a habit of writing down any side effects that I get, as and when I get them. Some of this makes for very unpleasant reading now but I am so glad that I took the time to do it.

LESSON FIVE - IT TAKES TWO

It is definitely a major benefit to have someone accompany you on every meeting you have with your specialist or doctor. Having another person in your corner, giving you love and moral support is an obvious advantage but more importantly it provides you with another pair of ears. When in the middle of the purple mist it is all very well thinking that you have heard everything that your doctor or specialist tells you but I can definitely confirm that you don't. That is why it is so useful to have your buddy, your back up with you. It is no surprise that all detective teams come in pairs.

None of us can process everything that we are hearing, in fact most of us never listen as well as we hear. Even with the best planning we all forget to ask everything we intended to ask and we regularly misinterpret some of the information we are given. Having someone else with you, on your side, means that you get the most value from meetings with specialists and doctors. It also means that you double the chances of understanding what the plan is, why it is being suggested, what to expect from it and what you need to do if it does not work out.

LESSON SIX - TWO EARS, ONE MOUTH

I cannot emphasise enough how useful I have found it to talk to other ITP sufferers. Whether it be on the various social media platforms, of which there are many for ITP sufferers these days, or at the many meetings I have attended at the ITP Support Association or Rare Disease UK. Learning from other people, listening to their experiences good, bad and sometimes uncomfortable helped me to better understand my illness and plan for how to handle the various treatments that I tried.

I always followed the "two ears, one mouth" principle of meetings. I have always believed that you learn more from other people if you use your mouth and ears in the proportion in which they have been allocated. So listen twice as much as you speak and that way you learn more. So whether I was discussing my illness with my specialist, health professionals or other ITP sufferers I would make a conscious attempt to listen intently and speak sparingly. So on that note, I will say no more !

LESSON SEVEN - FAIL TO PLAN and PLAN TO FAIL

Undoubtedly, most ITP sufferers, much like me, will be diagnosed completely out of the blue. Our enigmatic illness usually creeps up on us like a surprise Birthday party that we had no idea that our family might be planning for us. Awkward, unpredictable, irritating, frustrating and a nuisance, ITP is not the ideal illness for those of us who like our lives in the predictable category.

I found that a hugely important thing for me, once I had been diagnosed and had processed the fact that I really was purple, was to draw up a plan of action to live with it. I made it a priority to use my illness to take stock of my life, focus on the things that I really wanted to do and ditch the things that I didn't want cluttering me up. If there was one positive that I could attribute to my ITP, it was that it got me thinking properly about planning for the future. It is not to say that I didn't already have good life plans in place but there is nothing like an illness to focus the mind.

So I would absolutely recommend that sitting down with a completely blank sheet of paper is a good idea. The key thing to remember with any planning though is to make sure you stay flexible. Always leave some wiggle room. With the wobbly nature of ITP and the unpredictability of many of the treatments and their side effects, you absolutely cannot expect to stick rigidly to your plan. Leave some room for manoeuvre and allow for the odd detour.

It is vital to have a general outline of what you want to do but you have to be able to roll with the punches a bit. You will have to duck, dive , bob, weave and adapt your game plan along the way. Having ITP made that even more pertinent as I realised that you really do have to make the most of your time, especially any period of remission or being drug free. The uncertain nature of our mystery illness means that we never know when it will rear its' ugly head again. Having a plan to use our time well, seems to me to be a priority. If you haven't got a plan, get one.

LESSON EIGHT - LIVE YOUR LIFE

Planning what you want to do certainly focuses the mind but whatever goes into your plan I would certainly keep it based on the things, people and places that you really love. Do the things that you really want to do, go to the places you have longed to go to and include the people you really want to be with. I certainly took quite a while to come to terms with my condition and I wish that I had got to grips with it sooner. I think, on reflection that I did let it hamper me a bit too much in the early stages. I suppose that it is only natural with any illness, especially if, like me you have never had any ill health before.

I know that I became apprehensive and more cautious, probably overly so. I realise now that I could have been more relaxed about it much quicker but I guess we are all different. Obviously you have to exercise some caution and as with any medical condition it is important to discuss your own situation in full with your medical advisor BUT you have to live.

ITP cannot completely define any of us, it is just a part of us. It is easy to say "live your life" but I cannot think of any other way to express it. ITP is a tricky, intrusive, difficult condition and I would never underestimate the very serious potential the illness can have but eventually I got beyond that. I certainly realised that the most important thing was to keep busy, stay positive, remain optimistic and avoid dwelling on the negatives. Worrying about the things you cannot control or influence is a waste of time and energy. Equally using your time to ponder things that may or may not happen is just futile. Enjoy the moment and don't let your ITP steal your thunder !

LESSON NINE - TRY , TRY , TRY

It is very important to remember that with ITP there are numerous treatments available now. If the first one you have doesn't work there are many others still on the list. To put it another way, with ITP there may be many purple rivers to cross but there are now a lot of bridges to use to get over them.

You really do have to be persistent in your efforts to hold ITP at bay. It is very rare that any of us responds completely satisfactorily to just one single treatment. I have had steroids five times, Azathioprine, then Rituximab twice and now Mycophenolate Mofetil .

There have been plenty of turbulent times but you have to keep trying and eventually there will be a treatment that works best for you. I seem to have found my preferred drug in MMF whereas other sufferers will no doubt have settled on other options depending on their situation.

It is so easy to say but positivity and persistence eventually pays off. I had very little faith in that statement myself during my very worst moments but you have to keep on keeping on. There are plenty of keys to try to unlock the ITP door, albeit, at times it feels like you have not necessarily got the correct lock let alone the right key.

LESSON TEN - PUT the PRED to BED

No ITP discussion or list of purple lessons could ever be complete without mentioning steroids. The focus of any discussion for us ITP folk usually raises the ugly Prednisolone head at some stage. And so it is wholly appropriate that my final lesson should be devoted to our favourite subject.

Let's start with the positives from my point of view. I am one of the lucky ITP sufferers who does see a good response in my platelet count to steroids. Every time that I have taken Prednisolone my platelet count has gone up within a week. That is the end of the positives .

Sadly, the horrible side effects are the problem and for me they have created more difficulties than the ITP itself. From double chins to extra heft, from shingles to swollen knees, from aching joints to headaches, from sleepless nights to dozing days all are Prednisolone tales that will be familiar to most ITP sufferers.

If I were starting out on my ITP journey now, I would definitely not have taken Prednisolone as much as I have. After having steroid treatment on the first two occasions I would have declined it thereafter.

This is all so easy to say now of course. I fully appreciate that for some people steroids may well be the best and even the only treatment option that works. From my own case history I am certain that the awful side effects were just not worth it for me. After my second Prednisolone encounter, I should have put it to bed.

Thankfully I have now settled on Mycophenolate Mofetil which has worked well for me since April 2016 but it took five rounds of steroid to get there. I am not criticising any of the advice or treatment that I have been given but the impact of the steroids is something that I have already suffered too much from.

To conclude this chapter, I can only hope that other ITP sufferers will benefit from some of the lessons that I have learned along my purple journey. I have certainly come to realise that when it rains, it doesn't just fall on one person's house. ITP is a plague on all of our dwellings. Hopefully, by telling my story and sharing some of the harsh lessons that I have learned, it might just become a small part of someone else's survival guide.

CHAPTER NINETEEN

Starlings scoffed my Strawberries and Slugs savaged my Spinach

Just after being diagnosed with ITP, I had decided that I wanted to start growing some of my own fruit and vegetables. It took me a year or so thereafter to get going but, since 2008 my wife and I have been digging for victory. It has provided a wonderful antidote to my ITP. Our garden has been a great way to reconnect with nature, enjoy some fresh air, and get some exercise. In addition to all of that we have had some great fresh food and hopefully done our bit for the environment. I have learned a great deal too, not least that starlings love my strawberries and slugs regularly make a meal of my spinach.

I have leaned very heavily on a number of hobbies, interests and pastimes to divert my attention from my ITP since my diagnosis. I have already referred to my studies with the Open University in earlier chapters. Equally important for me has been music, both going to watch live performances and listening to it on vinyl, tape, cd or MP3. Reading and writing have also been wonderful ways for me to do something constructive whilst platelet counting.

On the horticultural front, we have worked very hard in convincing our modest, suburban garden to produce an amazing array of fruit, vegetables and flowers. It has been an incredible amount of work and has also been a great learning experience at the same time. We have gained a tremendous amount of gardening knowledge and it has greatly improved the quality of our lives. It has also been a sobering reminder that you don't have to spend money like a drunken sailor on shore leave, to get the most out of life. The simple things are often free and provide the most satisfaction.

I had always wanted to use some part of our garden to start growing some fruit and vegetables. With the usual time constraints of work commitments and myriad other excuses we had simply never got around to doing anything formal. Yes, we had landscaped the space nicely and had smart flower beds and our garden was providing plenty of colour and beauty. But, apart from a few herbs we had never tried to grow anything that we could eat. It was only in 2007 when we got a potting shed and glass house installed that we knew that we had no more excuses. It was now or never ! There would be no going back.

I had been inspired to try growing some of our own food, because I remember as a young boy helping my Grandfather in his garden where he grew plenty of fresh produce. He and my Grandmother had set up a very productive back garden in their suburban house during World War 2 and they also had an allotment. I suppose they did have Hitler and the Ministry of Food to motivate them, but it worked a treat. They were digging for victory so that we could dig for fun.

After the cessation of hostilities in 1945 my Grandparents continued in their garden as if the war never ended, although thankfully they did remove their Andersen shelter. They were very wise, they always enjoyed good, fresh food, They were determined that it would underpin their lives and those of their children and grand children, including me. I couldn't help but be influenced and inspired by them.

As an interesting side note, the irony is that during World War 2, even with the terrible food shortages and rationing that Britain experienced, our nation was far healthier than it is now. As of 2017 the UK is officially the fattest nation in Europe. We live in a country where over 2/3rds of us are either obese or overweight and it is getting worse. The steroids haven't helped me to improve those statistics by the way.

Anyway, back to my garden story. In Autumn 2007 whilst going through some old books in our loft, I discovered one of my Grandfather's old gardening text books. I had actually forgotten that I even had any of his old books so it was a huge surprise. Inside the book was also a seed catalogue dating back to 1959. The catalogue had a few hand written notes that my Grandfather had made next to the items that he had ordered. It brought a tear to my eye just to see those annotations but it was beautifully serendipitous.

The discovery of these items just seemed to confirm to me that it was right that I embark on my own growing project. In some ways it was like an affirmation that the time was right for me to emulate everything that my Grandparents had done before me. I guess that I saw it as a metaphorical "pat on the back " from them, especially from my Grandfather who was and has been one of the biggest influences on my life. I don't usually believe in things like "signs" or "it was meant to be's " but nonetheless it was a wonderful coincidence.

So I started to make plans, in earnest, for our garden project in the Winter of 2007/8 and I have kept a garden journal ever since. I have recorded our plantings, outcomes, successes, many failures and eaten some of the evidence. We have had numerous setbacks, lots of bruises, blisters and a few disasters. But it has been great fun and extremely rewarding.

We are very fortunate to have a south facing garden, so we get the warmest, sunniest weather that our very tricky climate offers. Although we constantly talk about the weather here in the UK, the truth is that we live in a very productive part of the World. Our climate is actually very, very temperate. We don't get the kind of dangerous, unpredictable weather that you find in some parts of the World, albeit we are getting erratic events (flooding , storms and wind) more often now than we have in the past. One of my Grandfather's favourite sayings was that there is no such thing as bad weather but there is the wrong clothing !

Having had our potting shed and greenhouse erected in Summer 2007, all we had to do to start our production was build 3 raised beds on the left hand side of our garden. That is the eastern side of the garden and gets the sunshine during the hottest part of the day. We needed 3 beds because it is important to rotate crops every year. You shouldn't plant the same crops in the same bed year after year, because pests and diseases get used to them being in that place and attack them. Moving crops to different areas each year means that it can minimise the impact of any potential predators. You can never beat every single pest but rotating gives you the best chance.

The trouble with growing your own produce is that the moment you have anything remotely edible it attracts various interlopers wanting their ration of it. So you have to be ready to combat the aphids, slugs, field mice, cabbage white butterflies, squirrels, hedgehogs, cats, birds and numerous plant diseases. You have to accept that you will lose some of your crop because you simply can't ward off all of the visitors, all of the time.

We learned that our fruit could be protected by netting but often nature is the best referee. For example our resident hedgehog family and toads and frogs from our neighbours pond clear up our slug problem and ladybirds reduce our aphid troubles. Nature has great ways of helping you out when it helps itself !

We decided to grow everything from seed, so the greenhouse comes into play every Spring usually in early March. It then remains stuffed full of developing pots of various crops at various stages of readiness right through until October. Once the seeds have sprouted and grown to a reasonable size, hardy enough to be transplanted to pots of their own, we move them into an outdoor covered area. They then get bigger and stronger before being transferred out into the big, wide World of the 3 raised beds. So from early May onwards we have produce in our 3 beds, maturing in readiness for our plates.

The whole enterprise has been great fun, albeit hard work. You really do only reap what you sow in this annual garden game. But we have enjoyed so many fruits and vegetables over the last ten years. Our greatest fruit successes have been, raspberries, loganberries, blackcurrants, strawberries , tomatoes and red currants. We had no luck with gooseberries.

On the vegetable menu we have done well with potatoes, peppers, chillies, garlic, onions, peas, beans, beets, Swiss chard, kale, lettuce, rocket, cucumbers, radish. We have been useless with celery, fennel, cabbage, spinach, courgettes. Herbs are fairly plentiful with basil, oregano, sage, chives, marjoram, thyme, mint being the easiest and most successful.

The key thing about the garden is that you never stop learning. There is always something new to try or a different pest that we hadn't expected that suddenly materialises. The most important part about it all is to remember to grow things that you really like and will actually eat. Temper all of this by making sure that you enjoy what you are doing and grow produce that you know does well in your garden. If something has not gone well in the past, the chances are that it may not go well if you try it again. Learn from previous mistakes but don't be afraid to have a go.

I am comforted by remembering something that my Grandfather once told me when I was much, much younger. It went something like this... "If you eat locally produced food, when it is in season, prepare it simply and don't mess around with it, then you will thrive. If you eat well, then you will live well ! " Wise words indeed and one's that I have always borne in mind. They are more prescient now than they were all those years ago. I am certainly not a preachy kind of person, but it all seems like common sense to me.

Our garden project has been a wonderful distraction from my ITP over the last ten years or so and it has had the added bonus of filling our plates, and our flower vases too. I can't pretend that it has been free from a lot of hard work. But you have to remember that if you do nothing, then you get nothing !

Despite all the setbacks nothing quite beats picking our first strawberries and raspberries of the season in June and adding them to our muesli for breakfast in the garden on a sunny day. Or a lunch with our new potatoes, dug up, boiled and eaten with butter and parsley or chives all within 10 minutes from them being in the soil.

It is also somewhat comforting to know that we can almost predict roughly what the garden will produce at the same time every single year. So May is Rhubarb, Rocket, Radishes, Primrose, Lily of the Valley, Bluebells. June is Strawberries, early Raspberries, Cucumber, Mint, Peas, early new Potatoes, Roses, Peonies and more Roses. July is Courgettes (with luck), Raspberries, Blackcurrants, Lettuce, Broad Beans, Basil, and so on all the way through until the end of November with each month having its' own signature produce. Wonderfully satisfying and equally remarkable.

One of my greatest pleasures in the Summer is getting up at around 6am and giving all of the plants and produce in our garden and the greenhouse a watering whilst listening to the birds in song. The smells and sounds of an English Summer morning are incomparable. Whether it is the waft of the Lily of the Valley in May, the heady scent of the Roses in June or the mix of thyme, rosemary, mint and basil as I brush past the herb garden.

All these things evoke other memories too, like recalling how my Grandmother's favourite flower was Lily of the Valley. Just getting a delicate waft of the perfume from that flower brings my Grandmother back to me.Wonderful memories even the one's of her scolding me to hurry in from the garden for tea, interrupting my carefully crafted Jimmy Greaves hat trick of goals against my cousin.

Even if the starlings have nibbled one or two of our strawberries and the slugs have dined on our spinach, we still have some produce left for our plates. After all we must remember that our garden is not just our little patch of England. We share it with plenty of other visitors who help to make it our home and their's too.

When all is said and done, it is not our house or garden at all. We don't actually own anything. Our names are on the title deeds and all the regular bills but we are just the current custodians, it will all be here after us. We can just hope that we tend it well, care for it lovingly and take from it only what we need. Hopefully we leave it in a better condition than it was in, when we arrived. It won't be for the want of caring or trying. It's what my Grandparents did and if it worked for them, it will work for us. It's common sense and we need that more now than we've ever done !

CHAPTER TWENTY

It Runs in the Blood

For us seasoned ITP campaigners one of the things we get used to pretty quickly is rolling up our sleeves to undertake regular blood tests. During my purple career, I would hate to estimate the number of times that I have had the needle. Obviously the only way to check the platelet count is by having a blood test but what else can our doctors or specialists possibly be looking at when they analyse our blood test results ? What other important information can they glean from a few test tubes of claret ?

In this chapter, I will break down the various things that I have learned that my specialist looks at when reviewing my blood test results. As with all things ITP, I would remind anyone reading this that these are the things that my specialist looks at with me. All of our cases are completely unique so what my specialist will look at may well be different to that which another specialist will investigate with another patient. Our individual medical histories , previous treatments, current drugs, age and other medical conditions will determine what our specialists, specifically want to look for.

One general thing to say about blood and blood tests is Water. What I mean by this is that something we can all do to help our blood is drink plenty of water. Keeping hydrated is so important. For starters it helps the phlebotomist get our blood sample easier. Basically if we are dehydrated it is more difficult for them to get a sample of our blood. It doesn't flow so to speak. Drinking plenty of water also means that our platelets will be less likely to clump. If our platelets do clump, it is difficult to get a clear platelet reading. The suggestion is that we should drink about 2 litres of water per day, so I am certain that we all have room to do more. Gulp !

My blood test of August 21st 2017 showed the following detail listed at the top of the print out of my results .

1. HB - 160 ,
2. WCC - 6.5,
3. NEUT - 3.00,
4. CREAT - 97,
5. LFTS - Normal
6. PLT - 205

What does all this mean, exactly what are the abbreviations and are the numbers good, bad, normal or concerning ? Before, I go on to explain them all in a bit more detail, I can say that the numbers were all good news. As to what they are, why they are important and what the specialists are looking for, I will try to explain.

1. **HB - 160**

HB is an abbreviation for Haemoglobin the protein in our Red blood cells which carries oxygen to our organs and tissues. It also transports carbon dioxide away from them back to our lungs. A lower than normal HB level means you have a low Red blood cell count and maybe Anemic. It means that your tissues and organs are not being oxygenated properly or carbon dioxide not expelled correctly.

What is a normal HB level ?

The normal HB range for men is 13.5 to 18.0 grams of Haemoglobin per decilitre of blood, and for women it is from 12.0 to 16.0 grams per decilitre of blood. In children the normal range varies depending on age. So my own recent blood test showed me at 160 meaning that at 16.0, I was exactly within the normal HB range for a man of between 13.0 and 18.0 grams of Haemoglobin per decilitre of my blood. So far, so good but what is a low HB level and why does it matter ?

What is considered to be a low HB level ?

This is generally defined as less than 13.5 grams of Haemoglobin per decilitre of blood for men, so expressed as a figure of 135, and 12.0 grams per decilitre for women, expressed as a figure of 120 in any blood test results. A low HB level may indicate that the patient has Red Blood Cell problems. Our bodies produce fewer Red Blood Cells than normal if any of the following conditions are evident - Aplastic Anemia, Cancer, using certain medicines such as anti-retroviral drugs for HIV infection, and treatments of Chemotherapy drugs for cancers and other conditions.

Why does an ITP specialist want to look at our HB count ?

Our specialists look at our Red Blood Cell count to check that in addition to our ITP there are no other problems with production of our Red Blood Cells and our general bone marrow health. Also where treatments for our ITP have been used, our specialist wants to confirm that these drugs are not be having a detrimental impact on our HB levels. Some of the drugs used to treat our ITP may have an impact on our ability to produce healthy Red Blood Cells so it is something our specialists will keep an eye on over time to check for any changes. Prednisolone can for example lower the Red Blood Cell count in some cases.

What are the symptoms of a low HB level ?

If the patient has a low HB level they may experience some or a combination of the following symptoms.

A. General Fatigue.
B. Weakness.
C. Pale skin.
D. Shortness of breath.
E. Dizziness.
F. Strange cravings to eat items that are not food (for example dirt, ice, clay).
G. Tingling or crawling feeling in the legs.
H. Tongue swelling or soreness.

A low HB level maybe experienced because of an iron deficiency which causes Anemia. Women in child bearing years are at a higher risk of suffering from iron deficiency because of blood loss during menstruation. Anemia can be caused by ulcers, cancer, use of some pain relievers such as Aspirin and heavy menstrual bleeding.

Can you have an HB level that is too high ?

YES - this is absolutely possible and is often experienced in patients who may have heart or lung problems. In cases of high HB levels the patient has Red Blood Cell production which is too high as it compensates for lower blood oxygen levels often reduced because of heart or lung problems. Another potential reason for high HB levels is a bone marrow dysfunction that results in increased Red Blood Cell production.

What does our body need to produce healthy Red Blood Cells ?

We need Folate and Vitamin B12 to enable our system to produce healthy Red Blood Cells. Folate is found in dark leafy green vegetables like spinach, kale, cabbage, broccoli. It is also found in asparagus, citrus fruits, lettuce, strawberries, raspberries, almonds, beets, celery, squash, carrots, corn, sprouts, peas and lentils.

Vitamin B12 is found in eggs, cheese, milk, meat, fish, poultry.

But like in all things a sensible, balanced, diet is the way to go. Obviously if you do have a low or indeed high HB level your specialist/doctor will discuss it with you and should suggest ways for it to be corrected/improved. It is very important to discuss any radical change you may be thinking about making in your diet with your specialist or doctor before doing so.

So having looked at the Red Blood Cell count attention turns colour to white.

2.   **WCC - 6.5**

WCC stands for White Blood Cell Count and it is a very important part of the analysis that our specialist will want to look at. White Blood Cells are a vital part of our immune system and they are also often referred to as Leukocytes. They help fight infections by attacking bacteria, viruses, germs and infections. White Blood Cells like our Red Blood Cells and Platelets are produced in our bone marrow.

There are several different types of White Blood Cell, the main one's being Neutrophils our most important White Blood Cells (more about them later), T-Cells and B-Cells.

What is a Normal White Blood Cell Count ?

White Blood Cells are measured in thousands per micro litre of blood. So my recent blood test produced a reading of 6.5 WCC which means 6500 White Blood Cells per micrometer of blood. The normal range of White Blood Cell Count is anything between 4300 (4.3) and 10800 (10.8), although slight variations on these figures may be seen at different laboratories/testing centres. So my recent reading of 6500 (6.5) is well within the normal, range and that of course is great. But why is it great and why does it actually matter ?

If our White Blood Cell Count is below the expected normal range or at the lower end of it, our specialist may wish to investigate further. A low White Blood Cell Count often referred to as Leukopenia, may be a concern because it means that our ability to fight infections, viruses, colds, flus, bugs of all sorts may be reduced leaving us vulnerable to illness.

A low White Blood Cell Count may be triggered by some autoimmune disorders, bone marrow disorders or damage, lymphoma, HIV, severe infections, liver and spleen diseases, lupus, radiation therapy and some medications like antibiotics. So our specialists will want to keep an eye on our White Blood Cell Count as it is a good indication of our overall health, our ability to fight infections and it may reflect any other issues apart from ITP that are going on.

It is also vital that the White Blood Cell Count is monitored closely after any treatment for our ITP as it may be impacted by some of those treatments (Rituximab for example can reduce the White Blood Cell Count).

But can you have a White Blood Cell Count that is too high ?

Oh yes indeed you can and this is called Leukocytosis. I had exactly this problem in Summer 2016, albeit this was a short lived spike in my White Blood Cell Count which I will explain a bit more later.

A high White Blood Cell Count can be triggered by smoking, infections like tuberculosis, tumours in the bone marrow, leukaemia, inflammatory conditions like arthritis, bowel diseases, stress, tissue damage, allergies, asthma, pregnancy and some drugs like...... wait for it .....some of you may have already guessed this one..... and BOOM !.......Corticosteroids our old friend Prednisolone (see more about this in the next item below headed 3. NEUT).

So how do we maintain a good level of White Blood Cell Count ?

Like our Red Blood Cells and Platelets the White Blood Cells are produced in our bone marrow, so it won't come as any surprise to learn that once again Vitamin B12 and Folate are important for our White Blood Cell production. Time and time again it is the old evidence of fresh fruit and vegetables and a healthy balanced diet that is the best general advice. Much of course depends on our personal medical history and any other medical conditions and drugs we may be taking or have taken in the past. We are all different but you can't escape the general vibe that fresh fruit, vegetables and avoiding fatty processed foods can only be good for us.

3. **NEUT 3.00**

NEUT is an abbreviation for Neutrophils and these are a type of White Blood Cell. They are actually the most plentiful of our white Blood Cells making up somewhere between 55 and 70 per cent of all our White Blood Cells. Neutrophils are especially important as they play a vital role in our immune systems and its' ability to fight infections, viruses, bugs, bacteria etc. Neutrophils circulate in our blood stream and when they sense signals that an infection is present in our bodies, they are the first cells to migrate to the site of that infection to start killing off the invading microbes, In essence they are our "first responders" so to speak.

So if we have got a good number of Neutrophils it is an excellent indicator of the overall health of our immune system and its' ability to fight off anything thrown at it. The Neutrophils in our blood are measured in a blood test and the specific test for them is known as the Absolute Neutrophil Count (ANC). The ANC is calculated by multiplying the White Blood Cell Count by the percentage of Neutrophils in the blood. A healthy Neutrophil count is between 2500 and 6000, so once again at my last blood test my reading of 3.0 (3000) is exactly where my specialist wanted it to be thank goodness.

So what else do we know about Neutrophils ?

Antigens are the substances which call our immune systems into action when we need them to help us ward off potentially harmful invaders like bacteria, viruses, poisons, fungi, cancer cells. Our immune system is made up of tissues, organs, and cells. It is our White Blood Cells which patrol our blood stream and lymphatic system and these White Blood Cells produce chemicals which attack and fight off harmful substances by going to the source of the infection or inflammation. OK that sounds fairly straightforward but what about the Neutrophils ?

Well our Neutrophils are so very important because and here is the key bit..... unlike the rest of our other White Blood Cells, they are not limited to a specific area of circulation. Our Neutrophils move freely through the walls of our veins and into tissues of our bodies to attack antigens (harmful stuff) quickly. Our Neutrophils are our key response team if you like, they can go anywhere, they can do what other White Blood Cells can only dream of doing. It's the unlimited, free movement that distinguishes the Neutrophils from the rest of the White Blood Cells you see, so they are absolutely the top white cell dogs.

Right then what happens if your Neutrophil count is low and why might that be ?

A low Neutrophil level is called Neutropenia and it can be caused by a suppressed immune system (for example long term use of steroids, or Rituximab treatment), some other drugs like chemotherapy, some conditions like aplastic anaemia, bone marrow failure, HIV, some autoimmune illnesses like rheumatoid arthritis, leukaemia, and some congenital disorders like Kostmann Syndrome and Cyclic Neutropenia.

Low levels of Neutrophils can be dangerous as it means we will be much more vulnerable to infections, bacteria, viruses, illnesses in general. If our levels fall below 1500 (1.5) Neutrophils per micrometer of blood this could be life threatening if we are then exposed to infection etc as our systems would struggle to fight it off.

So can you have a Neutrophil level which is too high ?

Oh yes indeed you can and such a condition is known as Neutrophilia. I have been one of those people with a higher than normal Neutrophil count. I alluded to it earlier and it happened to me back in the Summer of 2016. The reason why my Neutrophil levels were a bit too high was a direct response to my taking Prednisolone . So in my case there was an obvious and acceptable reason why my Neutrophil levels had increased. My specialist also knew that once my Prednisolone dosage was reduced we would see a corresponding fall in my Neutrophil level. And we did ! Three cheers all round and cup of tea for everyone !

A higher than normal Neutrophil level can be caused by infections (usually bacterial), non infectious inflammation, surgery, smoking, high stress levels, over exercising, heart attack, chronic myeloid leukaemia and as already stated, steroids including Prednisolone.

So our specialists want to keep a close eye on our Neutrophil levels and will investigate further if our results show anything which strays too far from the normal range, especially if there is no obvious explanation why.

Right so we've now looked at Red Blood Cells, White Blood Cells and the key White Blood Cell Neutrophils. What else is in the blood test that might be useful for our specialist ? Well next up is something called Creatinine.

4.   CREAT 97

CREAT is an abbreviation of Creatinine which is the waste product that our bodies produce from the normal breakdown of our muscle tissue. This break down product of Creatinine Phosphate in muscle is produced at a fairly constant rate by our bodies. Creatinine is filtered through our kidneys and excreted in our urine. The testing of our Creatinine levels is something which acts as an indicator of the efficiency of our kidneys and renal system.

What should our Creatinine level be then ?

Normal levels of Creatinine in our blood are between 0.6 and 1.2 milligrams of Creatinine per decilitre of blood for an adult male (expressed as between 60 and 120) and 0.5 to 1.1 in an adult female (expressed as 50 and 110). Figures for children depend on age.

When our Creatinine levels are tested our specialist is looking at the efficiency or otherwise of our kidneys and renal system to rid our bodies of this substance. If we have too much of it in our blood sample then it indicates that we are possibly having kidney or renal system issues in expelling it from our bodies. If we have too little of it then it could indicate that we may have an underlying reason for not producing enough of the Creatinine in the first place. Clear ? Well just to explain a bit more....

A higher than normal Creatinine level might mean what exactly ?

It could signify a problem with the kidney function or kidney disease /damage. In the event that our kidney function is hampered for any reason Creatinine levels in our blood will rise due to poor clearance of it by our kidneys. So we keep more of it on board than is normal, so to speak.

Our specialists will want to keep an eye on this because like many other aspects of our system, any treatments we have had for our ITP might produce a reaction in our kidneys and renal system. In most cases it will not cause any issues. My recent result of a Creatinine level of 97 confirmed that despite many different treatments for my ITP, everything is in order. Remember that I have had Prednisolone 5 times in my ITP years, Rituximab twice and Mychophenolate Mofetil.

High levels of Creatinine might be due to kidney or renal system damage or disease but also they could be the result of infection, major shock, low blood flow to kidneys, urinary tract blockage, heart problems, cancer and to round things off here's another of our old friends Dehydration (we need to drink 2 litres of water per day in case you'd forgotten).

Now low levels of Creatinine may also occur and indicate lower muscle mass caused by Muscular Dystrophy or ageing. (Basically as we get older we just have less muscle left). Pregnancy can also cause low Creatinine levels and low levels might also indicate some types of liver disease or a diet especially low in protein .

The mention of the liver leads me nicely into the next part of my recent blood test.

5. **LFT's**

The letters LFT stand for Liver Function Tests and they are a group of tests designed to give information about the general health of our Liver.

There are six Liver Function Tests which are usually conducted via the blood test, and they are … 1) Alanine Transaminase (ALT), 2) Aspartate Aminotransferase (AST), 3) Alkaline Phosphatase (ALP), 4) Albumin, 5) Total Protein, 6) Bilirubin.

Most Liver diseases cause only mild symptoms initially but diseases must be detected early. Our Liver is incredibly resilient and is the biggest internal organ in our bodies. The biggest organ incidentally is our skin. Our Liver is vital in detoxifying our bodies (getting rid of the substances and chemicals we do not need) and storing the chemicals and vitamins that we do need to maintain our health.

Our specialist will keep an eye on our overall Liver health because if we have any treatments for our ITP it could impact on the efficiency and condition of our Liver. In fact the Liver has a key role in the normal blood clotting process and if the Liver is damaged the blood becomes thin and takes longer to clot. A symptom of this is ….. DRUM ROLL …… a tendency to bruise easily.

Additionally for us ITP folk our specialist will keep a close eye on our Liver function because although in most ITP cases it is the Spleen where our Platelets are destroyed, the same can happen as a result of Liver damage.

The substance called Thrombopoietin is produced by the Liver and this is what regulates the production of Platelets. So any damage to the Liver may impact on the Platelets circulating in our blood if it hampers the production of Thrombopoietin.

So that's the offal bit over with and this all brings us nicely to PLT, the sixth part of my Blood Test results. You may well have guessed that this is Platelets. For us with ITP this is of course the heart of the matter. So here goes !

6. **PLT - 205**

So relief all round my Platelet count was 205, and this is confirmation that the Mychophenolate Mofetil that I have been taking since April 2016 was working. The dosage I had been prescribed had been reduced gradually since I started taking 750 milligrams, twice per day at the beginning. I was now on just 500 milligrams once per day and my specialist was hoping to reduce it to just 250 milligrams per day, then stop the dosage completely.

We would see soon enough if that worked but I can't say that I was not just a little sceptical that reducing the dosage too much might lead to the old purple ghoul returning.

It's a tricky balance, a choice that Hobson himself would think long and hard about. Nobody wants to take any drug unless they really have to but on the other hand the spectre of the old ITP looming large in the background was enough to keep me cautious about reducing my dosage too much too soon.

We all know that Platelets are the core of the ITP conundrum, so I won't rake over any more familiar, old ground here.

There are a number of other things that your specialist or doctor may request be tested when you have a blood sample taken. The following four are the most common. None of these are tests that I have had done but my specialist drew them to my attention as things that some people may encounter routinely.

1. Calcium Profile

A Blood Calcium Test is often used to diagnose/screen for conditions relating to the bones, nerves, heart , teeth and kidneys.

2. Urea and Electrolytes

Used to check kidney function.

3. Blood Film Examination

Shows information and detail about number and shape of red and white blood cells.

4. Lactate Dehydrogenase Level - LDH Test

http://www.nhs.uk/conditions/LDH/Pages/Introduction.aspx

This is used to check kidney and liver function. LDH is an enzyme the body uses during the process of turning sugar into energy for our cells to use. LDH is found in many of the body's tissues and organs, like the liver, kidneys, heart , muscles, pancreas, brain and blood cells. High levels of LDH may indicate tissue damage. Often our LDH levels are elevated after strenuous exercise.

I hope that this brief tour of my recent blood test has given a little insight into what our specialists may be looking at when they analyse our results and more importantly why they are looking at those things in the first place. Until 2006, I cannot remember ever having had a blood test in the first 46 years of my life. I'd just never been hors de combat at all, so blood tests were simply things that never happened to me.

So here's to the next sample of claret that I'm due to provide all too soon. Be sure that I'll be ready with my sleeve rolled up, well hydrated, prepared as ever for just a sharp scratch and hoping for the results to come back with the right numbers on them. All a bit of a lottery really but at least I now understand what the numbers actually mean.

The following links may be useful for anyone interested in finding out more information on the various tests.

CREATININE....
http://www.medicinenet.com/creatinine_blood_test/article.htm

LIVER FUNCTION TESTS...
https://patient.info/health/liver-function-tests

https://www.britishlivertrust.org.uk/liver-information/tests-and-screening/liver-function-tests/

https://www.healthline.com/health/liver-function-tests#uses3

BLOOD CALCIUM TEST...
https://labtestsonline.org/understanding/analytes/calcium/tab/test/

UREA and ELECTROLYTES TEST...
https://www.nursingtimes.net/clinical-archive/assessment-skills/why-do-we-test-for-urea-and-electrolytes/5067402.article

BLOOD FILM EXAMINATION...
https://www.medichecks.com/tests/blood-film-examination

http://www.medic8.com/blood-disorders/blood-test/specific-blood-tests/blood-film.html

LACTATE DEHYDROGENASE LEVEL...
http://www.nhs.uk/conditions/LDH/Pages/Introduction.aspx

CHAPTER TWENTY ONE

Banishing Ghosts of Christmas Past but Beware the Ides of March

The final throes of 2017 rushed by in a flash. It seemed like the last quarter of the year happened whilst I was making other plans. So once the ball had dropped again to signal another New Year, it was time to reflect upon my ITP state. The good news was that I was actually very much in the purple with platelet counts above normal, courtesy of my constant companion Mychophenolate Mofetil (MMF).

I really couldn't complain, as at my last three blood tests in 2017 my count read 205 on August 21st, 211 on October 25th and on 27th November 165. My specialist and I expected a slight drop in November as I had been suffering from a nasty cold the week before my blood test. So MMF had been working really well for me since I started out on it back in April 2016. I had very few side effects from it apart from being slightly nauseous (mainly in the morning an hour or so after taking the tablet) and a bit of trouble sleeping at night. But this was all standard apparently.

My specialist had reduced my dosage of MMF to only 500 mg per day which is very, very low indeed. I had started out on 750 milligrams of the drug twice per day and that is more like the dosage that I should have been taking in view of my size. At just 500 mg per day we were not actually sure if the MMF was doing anything at all. Perhaps my system had retrained itself or spontaneously gone into remission. Perhaps, perhaps, perhaps !

It was yet another of those purple conundrums.... Do we take away my best buddy MMF, knowing that the dosage was so small that it may not actually have been doing anything or do we just carry on with the 500 milligrams per day knowing that if my platelet count isn't broken then don't try to fix it ?

At the meeting with my specialist in November 2017 we had decided to just carry on with the current MMF regime. A dosage of 500 milligrams per day was tolerable with hardly any side effects and my platelets were as they should be, so why change anything ? There was no point in poking a wasps nest with a sharp stick was there ?

Like so many other ITP sufferers, I had fully understood that our enigmatic purple passenger needs no encouragement to rear its' ugly head. I was more than happy to leave things as they were. I was all for the status quo in this instance. But my specialist did suggest that he would like to take me off the drug at some stage. We would cross that bridge when we came to it.

So everything in my purple world had been quite settled throughout 2017 and I was just so grateful for that. It had enabled me and my wife and family to just get on with all the other problems and issues that life throws your way. It was a pleasure just focusing on being mundane and ordinary, so to speak. Sometimes we can forget how lucky we are when things are going well. We can very quickly set aside our bad memories or experiences once things start to go swimmingly well again. I was very much reminded of this during the Holiday Season of 2017 as my wife drew my attention to a Ghost of Christmas past. My itchy, shingles Yuletide of 2009.

It was hard to believe that during December 2009 I developed shingles as a result of having been taking Prednisolone, on and off from July 2006. Just thinking about the terrible pain that shingles caused me over that awful Christmas was like hearing the rattling chains of old Marley himself. It brought back horrible memories. It certainly was one of the most painful episodes of my ITP experience. The illness can be very dangerous so never underestimate it or the damage it can do. Thankfully though, Christmas 2017 went by without any purple incidents or itchy outbursts. I had thankfully banished some of those old ghosts.

So I was now well settled into my MMF regime and the plan we had agreed in November 2017 was that we would have no further visits to the hospital for check up's or blood tests until March 26th 2018 just a few days before Easter. I was to be checked every 6 months thereafter and remain on 500 milligrams of MMF for the time being. We would probably reduce my dosage to to 250 milligrams per day when I met my specialist in March. We seemed to have concluded that it may be best to leave me on the 250 milligrams of MMF from then on but like all things purple it was a matter of staying flexible. It was yet another semblance of a plan.

So with purple things relatively stable during 2017 we were able to focus on just living. We managed to get away for a week in September for example. A wonderful holiday in the Cotswolds was just so peaceful and what better part of England in which to spend an Autumn break ? We were blessed with clear blue skies and very warm, bright sunshine (Britain is often best in the Autumn, normally drier than Summer and although cooler, often clearer and brighter).

The Cotswolds is probably one of the most naturally beautiful places in Britain (certainly in England). The whole area is the picture of England that you might see on a chocolate box. Plenty of thatched cottages, tiny villages, stone buildings with a golden hue, log fired inns and history creaking from every rafter, nook and cranny.

One such charming place, Chipping Campden, is arguably the most beautiful and best preserved Medieval town in England. It is just so unbelievably pretty and charming. It is actually a living monument to the highly lucrative wool trade which took place between the 1400's and 1600's. Now the town is swamped with grazing tourists from May to August but the cuteness and beauty far outweighs the negatives. By visiting in September we were definitely seeing it at its' best with few other visitors to photo bomb any of our many pictures. We also enjoyed the charms of Broadway, Stow - on - the Wold, Cheltenham and Bourton - on - the Water that week. A real overdose of cuteness, with plenty of rest and relaxation.

In the late part of 2017 I was pleased to have been involved in the development of the ITP Pocket Log which is now available from the APP store. The Pocket Log has been developed by Novartis in association with the ITP Support Association. Having regularly used it myself , I can confirm that it is another very helpful ally in our coalition of forces against ITP. I was delighted to be invited to take part in the trials for the Pocket Log and can thoroughly recommend it to anyone of a purple persuasion.

You can download the Pocket Log for free and if you use it regularly as I do, you will find that it is a fantastic place to keep all of your important ITP records. It certainly beats carrying around bits of paper with scribbled, often illegible notes written hurriedly on them. I think most people will find it useful. I shared it with my specialist and he thought that it was brilliant. He promised to share it with all of his ITP patients, so hopefully it will be well received.

As I have mentioned in previous chapters, during my ITP years, I have had so many people tell me that they have never heard of ITP. However, I have also met many people who have said that they either have ITP themselves or know somebody who has it .

So on my visit to the Royal Berkshire Hospital for my check up in November 2017 it came as no surprise that the phlebotomist who took my blood sample knew a colleague in the same department who had ITP. Then whilst waiting to see my specialist, nursing a cup of Joe at the new and rather excellent coffee bar (can't resist the Danish apple cake) I got talking to another patient who has ITP. It is most definitely a small purple World.

Those chance meetings proved to me once again, that whilst ITP is quite rare, it is not as rare as it was when I started out on my purple journey. More is known about it, people who suffer from it are better informed about it and more willing to shoot the purple breeze too. In short, things are much better than they were and they are continuing to improve. We all have to be a part of that, we are our own best advocates and we can make a difference.

Fortunately not much happened with me on the purple front in the first two months of 2018 and I can only say that I was grateful that this was the case. So without anything alarming to report about my purple sidekick I accepted that no news in itself, had been a jolly good thing. We all realise that the last thing any of us ever want to do with ITP is tempt fate or goad it in any way. It was now over two years since my last purple outbreak and MMF had been my saving grace.

Some ITP sufferers have had equally positive responses from MMF but as ever all I can say is that like all treatments, responses vary. I continued to have excellent platelet numbers, and as previously mentioned my counts were well over 150 for most of 2017. I had no scheduled hospital visits due until March 26th. I continued to keep a watchful eye out for any unprovoked bruises and am always wary about any signs of over tiredness.

You have to keep a secret service like watch out for any ITP warning signs. That is the daily routine of any ITP sufferer, so nothing new there. The only side effects or noticeable problem I continued to get with MMF was a bit of nausea occasionally and this only seemed to last for about half an hour after breakfast. Inconvenient but manageable.

A slight frisson of excitement surrounding my MMF occurred when I asked my specialist if there is a suggested "best" time during the day when one should take the prescribed dosage. Goodness me, I might as well have asked him if he could give me the winning lottery numbers for the weekend. Never a straight answer you see. My question had been provoked by a number of comments from other MMF users on various ITP social media platforms.

They had variously suggested that it is best to take your medicine before a meal, after a meal, during a meal, two hours before a meal, even two hours after a meal to avoid any nausea or feeling of sickness. Well as ever with anything ITP, nothing is ever straightforward. There is no recommended time according to my specialist. It is, as ever, what works best for the individual. So trial and error really, but typically for ITP, wholly indiscriminate.

It is so strange being in remission because it not only alters my physical and medical condition but it allows for the restoration of my positivity. By nature I am an optimist and have always believed in the importance of recognising the best in people and all situations. But ITP really does impact upon all of that. I know that during my purple outbreaks I become much more defensive, cautious, worried and negative. All of that may well have had as much to do with having five separate rounds of Prednisolone treatments as the ITP itself.

Nevertheless with plenty of platelets on board, I had been getting on, with getting on. One of my New Year resolutions for 2018 was to see more films at the cinema. I promised myself and my wife that we would try. We have both always been movie fans but somehow the old ITP spoiler often interrupted that. But into 2018 and we were back on the overpriced popcorn.

There were some great films in early 2018 and I can thoroughly recommend *The Post*, *Finding Your Feet*, *The Greatest Showman*, *The Guernsey Literary and Potato Peel Pie Society*, but above all of them *Phantom Thread* with a fantastic performance by Daniel Day-Lewis. Set in Fitzrovia and the West End of London in the 1950's it puts Daniel Day-Lewis in the lead role of Reynolds Woodcock a pedantic, fastidious, childish, needy, genius dressmaker and designer. It is truly magnificent and definitely worth the entrance fee.

I had also been spending some of my free time tracing back my family history. It is something that I had always wanted to do and promised myself that I would devote some time to. I think as we get older we all start to wonder a bit more about where we have come from, where our origins really lie and how we arrived where we are now. I have been quite surprised by some of the things I have found and like most people discovered some good, bad and quite ugly in my story.

Some of the family that I thought I would have trouble tracing turned out to be quite easy to find and conversely some of the people I believed would be straight forward were as illusive as a Brexit deal. I knew that my paternal Grandmother was of Italian origin but I managed to trace her family back to Lake Como. Her ancestors fled from Napoleon and his army when they invaded Northern Italy in 1796. So somehow my Italian connection reached London in 1797, pitching up in Endell Street, Covent Garden. Small World, as that is just 5 minutes from where I was born.

On the wider ITP front, there were a few encouraging items of news. The first concerned three of the UK's leading ITP specialists who received grants from the BMA Jon Moulton Award to further their research into ITP. Dr Nichola Cooper, Dr Charlotte Bradbury and Dr Quentin Hill, all three directors of ITP Clinical Centres were worthy recipients.

The second piece of good news was the announcement of a Bristol and Wales ITP patient day to be held on the 27th April at the University Hospital of Wales. This was all part of the goal of encouraging more "local' ITP meetings and support groups to hold regular gatherings in the regions around the UK. Many more such local get togethers have happened since then. The ITP Support Association have been driving this initiative, adding their support and expertise to proceedings.

Finally, we marked another Rare Disease Day with the annual Rare Disease Day House of Commons reception held on February 28th. The theme was *Show your'e rare, show you care* . Although I couldn't make it to the House of Commons reception which I have attended five times out of the last six years, I would encourage anyone who has the chance to attend, to do so. (Receptions are held in England, Scotland, Wales and Northern Ireland and details are available from the Rare Disease UK website). If you cannot attend one of the annual receptions or many events, do get involved by just joining Rare Disease UK (which is free). It really helps.

I didn't have any further ITP check up's until March 26th so hopefully I was not going to be subjected to anything action packed or purple but even when writing in my diary about the events of early 2018, I was actually telling myself "don't tempt the purple fates". I almost knew what would happen if I did. I'd had plenty of experiences with ITP striking back just when the sailing was plain, so I really should have known what was coming. I ought to have listened to my inner purple radar and remembered that goading my ITP only ends badly. And so it proved.

As Julius Caeser said before his assassination, "the ides of March are come". It was one of the final things that he uttered and it added more weight to the warnings about the month before April as being one to approach with extreme caution. Like dear old Julius, I didn't see any danger coming but for me the month of March 2018 was a disaster. Everything was going so well until I was struck down with a terrible virus on March 4th. The full coughing, spluttering, wheezing, sneezing, feverish bug confined me indoors for over 2 weeks. I only left the house once to stock up on more paracetamol, lemons, honey, ginger, tissues and then for my hospital check up. Not for the first time, my wife did everything else.

Now I fully realise that a virus of this nature is hardly the end of the World and is probably just a turbo charged cold, but as we all know, taking MMF for ITP to control the platelet count effectively means that the immune system is very vulnerable to any bugs, flus; viruses, infections. If any of us happen to pick up any of these illnesses it is much more challenging for our immune system to fight them off.

Any ITP sufferer on any immune suppressing drug like MMF, Prednisolone, Rituximab , Azathioprine will know how difficult it is for the immune system to repel such bugs. It is like trying to roll a pea up a very steep hill or like having to run in treacle. Recovery from common illnesses takes much longer and it is one of the dangers of taking immune suppressing drugs to control our ITP.

As if a rotten virus was not enough, I also got another unwelcome surprise. During my ITP years I am constantly amazed by the incredible array of things that the wretched illness comes up with. When you think that it has thrown everything at you and that it can't really surprise you any more than it already has, that's when another rabbit comes out of the old purple hat. Having experienced swollen knees, inflamed ankle joints, shingles, nausea, dizziness, falling down my own stairs from top to bottom, being so sick I couldn't even speak, surely there wasn't much else in the old ITP play book. Wrong !

This time to keep my rotten cold/virus company I developed an awful, itchy rash all down both sides of my torso. My first thought was that the shingles that I'd had at Christmas 2009 may have returned. Perhaps I hadn't fully banished that particular ghost after all. Shingles (actually the chicken pox virus which stays in your body forever once you have had it) tends to reactivate (although not always) whenever the immune system is run down or suppressed. But I hadn't contracted shingles this time, thank goodness. The red spot explosion turned out to be a heat rash.

Because I had such a rotten cold/virus the fever that it generated made my body overheat. When the body generates excess heat, it produces sweat which basically then cools us down by getting rid of that heat. Because I had so much heat it resulted in a lot of sweat which blocks the sweat glands in the skin and traps the sweat/heat. So the skin produces red botches, blisters, spots and it manifests itself in a very sore, itchy rash. Charming.

After about a week the heat rash simply went down, albeit not without a a rotten irritable fight. As the virus got beaten and my body cooled down, my nuisance red pest dissipated. The only thing I could do to ease the itchiness and soreness of the heat rash was apply calamine lotion and wait for it to recede. The heat rash finally went away and my rotten cold cleared up too. Oh joy !

What luck for me then that it was all gone just in time for my blood test and hospital check up on March 26th. Having taken MMF for almost two years with brilliant results I still dreaded returning to the hospital. It wasn't just because the queues at the hospital are longer every time and parking fees higher with each visit but also that having had a wretched March chock full of illness, I was convinced that my platelet count was bound to have fallen.

Well, well, well my platelet count confounded me and my specialist. The vital number was 159 so still "normal" despite all the ides of March. My specialist was as surprised as I was that the platelet number was as good as it was given the nasty virus I'd had. He also reiterated that my dosage of 500 milligrams per day of MMF was so low that he was pretty sure it was probably not having any impact on my platelet count. My daily drug taking was probably no longer really needed. But as ever with ITP we could not be completely sure. We had already thought that this might be the case when I had been checked up in November 2017 so what next ?

Well the way forward was for me to stop taking MMF completely. I can't say that I was not just a little apprehensive about coming off the drug. I mean after 2 years on MMF with platelet counts well within the "normal" range, should I try to fix something that wasn't broken ? My specialist explained that taking MMF even at the very low dosage of 500 milligrams per day still had risks that we'd like to avoid if we possibly could.

As ever with ITP or any illness for that matter, any treatment is a balance of risk versus reward. The problems with MMF of suppressing the immune system which exposes the patient to potential serious illness had been all too evident in my own case. Also MMF can make the user more vulnerable to skin cancers so avoiding the sun (if we ever get any) is a very important thing for folk like me. Factor 50 and a hat at all times in Summer is my essential kit.

So as my specialist was fairly sure that the dosage of MMF I had been taking was too low to be having an impact on my ITP, then I would stop my MMF. We could assume that my immune system had probably, re-set itself (with the aid of the MMF) and effectively I could be completely drug free. This would be the first time I'd have been completely absent of narcotics for nearly 12 years. So by the end of April I was to give up MMF (hopefully for good).

Thereafter I would take nothing but then have a blood test to check the platelet count at the end of May. Hopefully the count would hold up but if it showed any signs of falling then I could always start back on the MMF if needed. I was sceptical as any ITP sufferer would be. That said I fully accepted that my current dosage was so low that I couldn't really understand how it was sufficient to be doing anything.

I could not pretend that I liked taking MMF, not least because it exposed me to more colds/viruses. Additionally of course it costs money to buy the drugs and time to visit the pharmacy to collect them. But nonetheless, giving them up was a big step, it was a risk and tempted the purple fates. Only time would tell if I could manage without MMF but in the meantime I was determined to keep a close eye on any potential return of the familiar symptoms. My daily check for bruises became a little bit more thorough but that's the nature of being an ITP sufferer isn't it ? It's part of the purple instruction manual.

CHAPTER TWENTY TWO

Snakes and Ladders

It is always a challenge to come up with a new phrase to describe the latest episode in my ongoing ITP journey. It's like trying to drink champagne from a flask of tea. As all purple sufferers know only too well, and as we have seen throughout this book, something always seems to come along to disturb your relative calm just when you least expect it. All the way through my ITP journey, numerous hazards have littered my purple road and nothing ceases to amaze me now. So it will come as no surprise to most ITP folk to know that in Spring and Summer 2018 just when I thought that I could be comfortable, the old purple monster decided otherwise.

The traditional, family game of Snakes and Ladders is the perfect analogy for those 4 months of my ITP journey. A game of chance, with unpredictable twists, turns, climbs, slips and slides. The ladders taking me high and then the hissing, snapping snakes tugging me back down.

As I explained in the last chapter, I actually started the Spring on the highest rung of the ladder with a real bounce in my step. At the end of March my Platelet count was at 159, everything going swimmingly well. We decided that as I was only on a modest dosage of MMF it was unlikely to be doing anything to support my Platelet count. At the level of my daily MMF tablet of 500mg it shouldn't have been worth a hatful of crabs. I might as well have been taking a Tic-Tac (apparently).

Let's try to put my low MMF dosage into perspective by saying that it was so low that it would be like giving an elephant a thimbleful of whisky and expecting to get the said elephant inebriated. As an aside, I wouldn't want to be the person holding the thimble. For a patient like me with my age and size taken into account, a daily dosage of 1500 mg of MMF would be the suggested appropriate amount. So the fact that I had been taking 500mg per day from Summer 2017 until March 2018 keeping a Platelet count over 150 and often over 200, made me something of a medical miracle.

So both me and my specialist, concluded in March 2018 that surely, all logic suggested that at only 500mg per day, the MMF couldn't be anywhere near enough to be doing anything ? Surely my system was coping and could manage without the MMF at all ? Well, sadly giving up the drug really put the tuba among the flutes. Now we all know that the word logic should always be used tentatively when mentioned in the same sentence as ITP. It's usually worth having a large pinch of salt handy. And so it proved in Spring 2018 with me and my purple.

As agreed, I gradually reduced the 500mg daily dosage of MMF to zero. By April 22nd I took no further drugs. My Platelet count would surely carry on at good levels without the drug. My immune system must surely have gone back to its' pre purple state. A factory re-set so to speak. How could it have been deriving any benefit from just 500mg of MMF, a mere thimbleful ?

Well, because ITP is ITP, of course it had to defy all logic and all our assumptions. I knew it probably would, I had a hunch all the long but of course we all crave a drug free existence and like to think the best. Sadly within 2 weeks of giving up the drug, my Platelet count fell to 60. I had slipped down the inevitable snake. From being atop the ladder on March 29th, I hit snakes tail on May 4th.

I knew that something was amiss because I had started to feel very tired about a week after giving up the drug. I also started to feel completely out of sorts, tetchy, irritable and distracted. Then I got a couple of bruises on my left arm, just above the wrist and another appeared completely unprovoked on May 3rd. They were sinister enough, and suspicious enough for me to go to the hospital to get a blood test straightaway. We purple people know how it goes. If in doubt, get checked out. Sure enough my Platelet count showed at 60. At that level it doesn't usually mean bruising of the unprovoked kind, so the bruises I had were probably small blows or knocks I had given myself. Even so, with all the tiredness, it was already pretty clear, that with no drugs, my Platelets would fall.

The drug free experiment lasted only 2 weeks. On May 6th I started back on MMF, this time at 500 mg twice per day to give my system a quick readjustment. We didn't want to risk the platelet count falling any lower. I was clearly going to be drug dependent for the foreseeable future, probably for the rest of my life. It was quite something to get my head around really, especially as the full implications just creep up on you don't they ? I mean, 12 or so years ago when I started out on this Snakes and Ladders game, I'd never taken any medication in my previous 46 years apart from paracetamol. Now I'm a regular at the local pharmacy and on first name terms with the staff.

You go from steroids for a three month hit to dampen the old immune system, to very serious drugs like Rituximab, Azathioprine and MMF just to pacify the purple, when in the past you were reluctant to take a pain killer for a toothache. The full implications of ITP just kind of absorb you, they can become your story if you let them. Our job as ITP patients, of course, is to let our illness just be a small part of our lives. Hopefully we can advise other people about it but don't let it be our whole story. It's an important chapter but it's not the whole book.

Back on the drug then and a slow climb back up the ladder. Hopefully a return to 500mg of MMF twice per day could steady things down and restore my platelet count to somewhere near normal levels fairly quickly. My specialist even hoped that once the platelet count had got back to normal levels we could reduce my daily dosage back to just the 500mg per day that was sufficient until we took me off the drug altogether.

Indeed everything did go according to plan. My count went back up to 120 within 2 weeks of going back on the drug at 500mg twice per day. With such a good response the dosage was then reduced back to just the 500 mg per day on June 25th 2018, when my count was 101.

Well, well, well, surprise, surprise. Fasten your seatbelts, purple turbulence incoming. Here we go again, time to buckle up and ride out the storm. As ever with our enigmatic condition, you are never far away from the next problem, and so it came as absolutely no surprise when I received yet another purple shot across my bows. Sceptical to have reduced my dosage so quickly, sadly I was proven right as my counts had reduced back to 78 on August 8th. So we instantly increased my MMF dosage up again to 500mg twice per day. We had embarked on a new game of chasing platelets.

Now don't get me wrong, I was very pleased to have a decent, safe count of 78, and I fully appreciate that many ITP sufferers would be ecstatic to reach such giddy heights. But the hassle, time wasting and general frustration at having your counts bounce around has its' own unsettling element. It was especially annoying this time, because if I hadn't come off the drug back in March/April, I would have been fine. It reinforces yet again that if your ITP isn't broken then don't try to fix it. Once you find the treatment regime that works for you, then unless the side effects become dangerous or threatening in other ways, do not deviate from it.

As ever it is the hassle, uncertainty and time consuming bit of ITP that is always so annoying. A visit to the hospital for a blood test means practically getting up in the middle of the night because I need to get to the blood test clinic by 7: 00am. It is so crowded all day from 7:30am to 5pm that unless you arrive half an hour before it opens you will wait in a queue for at least 2 hours.

Now waiting for any length of time at a hospital with perhaps 70 people ahead of you is not just frustrating and time wasting but it is the fastest way to get ill. If like some of us ITP folk, you are on an immune suppressing drug like MMF or steroids then of course it makes you more vulnerable, as I could testify. The best or should it be worst place to find viruses and bugs is a hospital. Surrounded by so many people waiting in a small reception area is not good for one's health. All of that is made even worse by the fact that the hospital is always far too hot and there is a lack of fresh air. In short it is the ideal place to get ill.

Anyway, as all ITP sufferers will attest, falling platelets just bring back the old nervousness. It adds a bout of wobbled collies and bumpiness to our journey. As highlighted many times already, when my numbers are falling I can feel that something is not right because I get so tired and generally out of sorts. I also find that I can't think straight, and that I take ages to do quite simple things. I have trouble focusing on routine tasks and easily lose concentration. I also get a bit clumsy, dropping things, fumbling and fiddling with simple items. I wouldn't make a good juggler !

It is hard to explain to anyone who hasn't suffered ITP or many other auto immune illnesses but I can only liken it to a deflated balloon at a Birthday party. You are completely down when you should be up. ITP has a habit of snuffing out your candle. The illness makes you low when everyone else is high. In short it's a complete party pooper.

What a rotten illness ITP is and it shows how difficult it is to get any treatment regime right even when you do find the drug that suits you. Once again, and I have no hesitation in repeating this - if you find the right drug and the correct dosage to treat your ITP, then do not change it. Do not try to get too clever. Stick, do not twist because you might just bust.

On September 24th 2018 when I met my specialist again, thankfully my platelet count was at 118 and we both concluded that I will remain on 500 mg of MMF, twice per day. That regime will probably now carry on for the foreseeable future, even possibly for the whole of my life. No more gambling or fiddling with my dosage. But as ever with ITP, who really knows ? The only thing we can be certain of is that my ITP will remain unpredictable, uncertain, tetchy, annoying and stubbornly difficult. Plus ca change ! But we carry on, carrying on. It's the only way we know.

In January 2019 I started out on my 13th ITP year and accepted that my enigmatic condition will always be with me. Thankfully I remain in remission at present, with a platelet count of 159 on March 29th. MMF has become my closest ally but it is possible that the purple ghoul may return. But then again it may not. No use worrying about it, because it just wastes time and energy. If you can't control it, don't worry about it. Sounds simple but it isn't quite like that is it ?

Almost inevitably my next appointment at the hospital to meet my specialist is to be on exactly the same day, to the day, on the 13th anniversary of meeting my ITP specialist for the very first time. Yes July 31st will see me back in exactly the same place as I was at the outset of this ITP adventure. I will be at the Royal Berkshire Hospital having a blood test, crossing my fingers that my platelets are behaving. The familiar routine. But, how time has flown and what testing times ITP has given me.

Even so, the key message for me, as ever, is to get on with life, do the things you want to do, see the things that you want to see, listen to music you love, be with the people that really matter to you. I have emphasised that message many times throughout this book but I find that constantly reminding myself about it is just as important now as it was way back when I started out on my ITP journey.

Whatever happens I will always be an ITP sufferer, the purple elephant never leaves the room completely but I have learned to live more comfortably with it. I am grateful that I have been able to eventually manage my illness. In spite of everything that it has thrown at me, I have come come through it with a number of tangible successes and achievements to my name.

The only place that I can really end my tale is by going back to the very beginning and addressing the question that all ITP sufferers ponder. So I will complete my ITP story with what I have come to consider the most important episode in all of my purple journey. Like most ITP sufferers I have constantly asked myself and my specialists "Why Me ? " It is the million dollar question isn't it ?

Looking back through the wonky, distorted lens of time, the following chapter presents my own answer to that question. It's just my theory but in the continued absence of any better explanation I'm sticking with it. I believe that I've finally reached the heart of the matter and in so many ways it has provided me with something of a closure of sorts. Read on and you will probably understand why.

CHAPTER TWENTY THREE

Once I was Seven Years Old

Like most ITP sufferers I have spent a good few hours contemplating how I developed this mysterious illness. As mentioned in previous chapters, I had never been seriously ill in my first 46 years. Apart from a few stitches to patch up football injuries I had never attended a hospital. Like most people I had suffered some nasty colds, and viruses over the years and one bout of bronchitis when I was 19 but nothing that could have provoked an outbreak of purple . So what made ITP rear its' ugly head ? Did I do something to provoke it ? Was the development of my ITP the result of an obvious incident which might be associated with immune system illnesses ?

Like all the great thrillers and mysteries they have to end with a solution don't they ? From Poirot and Marple to Holmes and Watson the best part is always left until last. I cannot pretend that my story is anything like as suspenseful as *Murder on the Orient Express* or *The Hound of the Baskervilles*. It's nothing like the butler did it with the candlestick in the drawing room. But nevertheless, I do have a purple solution. We have at last reached, the denouement and the heart of the matter, as far as I am concerned. Here's the big reveal. Over to you Sherlock !

During the last thirteen years, I have gradually developed my own theory about what actually set off the mayhem in my immune system. But the difficulty is, that even with the help of some of the most eminent ITP specialists I just cannot prove any of it. Supposition does not cut any ice in ITP. However, I personally believe that what triggered my immune system to go wonky was grief.

I am convinced that grief is the straw that broke the camels back in my immune system. I think that a combination of work related stress and a sudden bereavement of a very close family member in early 2004 was the trigger for everything purple to explode. My immune system treason came out of the blue but clearly it had been plotting for ages.

Now it is absolutely true that there can be no scientific evidence to support my claim. It is impossible to really understand what goes on inside our bodies/systems when we are under duress and emotional strain. I believe that I have a very high tolerance for stress, but in some senses that in itself may be unhelpful. Some people, like me are good absorbers. We bear our burdens lightly (at least on the surface). We may well defer a reaction to things like bereavement, duress, strain or shock. We are good at deflecting and solving problems but is that always good ?

Let me try to explain what I think happened to me. I believe that in early 2004 the death of a very close relative set off a response to that terrible shock in itself, but it also unlocked stored up emotional baggage that I had been carrying around with me since my childhood. This was excess luggage that I had been hauling around for nearly 40 years. This may seem hard to believe, but bear with me.

I think that the grief and shock that I could not process properly when I was just 7 years old when my Dad was killed in a tragic accident, was suddenly released or at least re-activated when I had news of the death of my uncle in 2004. So, the tragic death of my Dad all those years ago, was the event that I just never processed or accepted until eventually it forced me to confront it later in life. ITP was the ultimate response, albeit a very, very late one. Delayed grief was responsible for letting my ITP cat out of the bag and there was no chance of ever putting it back. My body finally said a resounding NO, I will not allow you to hide your grief any longer !

Now that is just my hypothesis and no ITP specialist can ever confirm how much of a bearing that delayed grief may have had in me becoming purple in 2005/2006. It may or may not be a factor. It's just my theory, my version of events if you like but something that I truly believe, eventually led me down a purple road.

Having said all that, I do not state this theory without having some back up evidence. My own experience of dealing (or not dealing with) grief is highlighted by Doctor Gabor Mate in his excellent book *When The Body Says No - The Hidden Cost of Stress* . He gives a great insight into the links between ill health and stress, trauma, emotions and environment. He demonstrates the importance of taking account of the mind - body link and the role that stress and our emotional make up, play in an array of diseases such as arthritis, cancer, diabetes, heart disease and numerous autoimmune illnesses, including ITP.

So much of what Dr Mate reveals definitely rings true of my own life story. He shows how the experiences we encounter in our childhood impact greatly on our adult lives. He explains how responses to those experiences inform the behaviours we learn and persist with in adulthood. Such behaviours and patterns are very difficult to break and we often go through life without realising that such traits may be harmful. Quite often we don't even recognise the behaviours at all because they simply become our reality. It just becomes what we do. So in my case, I learned to hide my grief because it was too painful to confront it. I carried on regardless.

In many ways my experience throws an astonishing amount of credence behind the theory that if you show me the child at seven, I will show you the man ! Could anything be more prescient in my case ?

I recognised so much about myself as I read and listened to Dr Mate. As he links childhood trauma, including bereavement and illness with ill health and even addiction in later life, very large bells began to toll for me. He demonstrates how our immune systems do not act in isolation from our daily experiences. We have to take a holistic approach to understand how our mind-body-immune system responds and in turn how it then impacts our health, both long and short term.

To attempt to explain his work fully in this book is not the correct platform to do so and it would be impossible to do it justice. However, there are numerous links to his work available free of charge on *You Tube* and he has published a number of books. He has undoubtedly helped me to better understand my own situation.

One of the key areas that Dr Mate focuses on is the fundamental need that we all have as children for attachment. He argues that the quality of the attachment that we enjoy in childhood with our parents, determines how we develop as adults and how safe and grounded we feel. This in turn influences how we ourselves then deal with the World. Basically he asserts that the more that we feel unconditionally loved in childhood, the more likely it is that we will deal well with the stresses and strains of the World around us later in life. Anything that interrupts that attachment with our parents/family, such as abuse, bereavement, divorce, family break up/separation, illness will impact greatly on our childhood and development especially if it is in our first 7 years of life.

Now as attachment is one of our fundamental, basic needs for the sake of survival, a child has no choice but to conform to an adults demands. So if necessary, the child will overlook his/her needs in order to obtain the approval needed from adults to guarantee survival. If a child makes this kind of compromise and adjusts his/her behaviour, he/she may well become an adult re-enacting the same pattern (mostly unconsciously) in any relationship and situation he/she is going to face. He/she is not likely to be able to say no, even if his/her basic needs are not met while constantly pleasing others more than is good for him/her. So at some point the body is likely to say no by triggering an illness. And boom, in my case, along comes ITP. It is almost as if ITP was saving me from myself.

Now none of this means that anyone going through these complicated behavioural patterns is a bad person or is somehow wrong. Quite the contrary in fact, because such patterns are completely natural responses to things like childhood bereavement, abuse, illness. The trouble is that we don't really even consciously recognise that we are adjusting our behaviour. Much less do we realise that such behaviour just becomes the way we are, it is just what we do, it is us !

Now, I always firmly believe that in life you have to look at the BIG things that have a had the most impact on you. Nothing in my life could ever be as big as the tragic, premature death of my Dad. I never processed it (nor was I encouraged to process or deal with it) at the time. I was deemed to be too young. So consequently, I believe that it lay dormant, ready for recall later in life. One truism about coming to terms with the death of a loved one, is that grief is like a fingerprint, it is unique and highly personal. In terms of Dr Mate's work he would suggest that my suppressing my grief meant that I adapted my behaviour at the time simply to survive. But in doing that, I stored up inevitable trouble for later in life. He is correct.

As Dr Mate explains…"Emotionally draining family relationships have been identified as risk factors in virtually every category of major illness."

"For the child it is no relief to feel sadness or anger if no one is there to receive those emotions and to provide some comfort and containment."

"When early environmental influences are chronically stressful, the developing nervous system and the other organs... repeatedly receive the electric, hormonal, and chemical message that the world is unsafe or even hostile. Those perceptions are programmed in our cells on the molecular level. Early experiences condition the body's stance toward the world and determine the person's unconscious beliefs about themselves in relationship to the world."

Now, looking back to that awful day in 1967 when my Dad was killed it has to be remembered that the World was a very, very different place then. I was never really allowed to grieve properly after his death. I was not permitted to attend his funeral. It was not deemed suitable for me to go, my family firmly believed that they were protecting me by blocking my attendance. I remember very little about the whole set of circumstances but do recall a host of unusual happenings. I was shielded from the reality of the situation. Rightly or wrongly, I never got exposed to the truth and so never processed anything about it. I deferred it all !

It was all just completely bewildering for a young boy still in short trousers. I just wanted to be Paul McCartney or Bobby Moore and be like every other 7 year old. I just cannot really remember much more detail. I do know that my entire family were completely distraught although they tried to shield their feelings and emotions when I was around. Looking back now, my confusion, grief and lack of coming to terms in full with matters is all perfectly understandable when considered in the context of that far away era. Undoubtedly bottling up emotional trauma from that time was basically storing up trouble for a future date. It was only postponing the outpouring of emotions and certainly not cancelling them.

But the considered thinking about such things back in 1967 was very much governed by values and ideas reflective of Victorian Britain. The stiff, upper British lip, was the only thing on the menu. It was all very John Mills, Trevor Howard and David Niven back then. The general attitudes to young people in so much of Britain in the sixties may be summed up by phrases like "children should be seen and not heard", "children should speak only when they are spoken to". These are all Victorian imports of course, straight from a Dickens novel. Now my family could never be considered staid or conservative but even so, the huge cultural, attitudinal and social changes that were heralded in during the sixties were still struggling to gain a sure foothold in 1967.

Things were just so different and a good sense of what the UK was like at that time is very well documented in the wonderful book by Shawn Levy - *Ready, Steady, Go !* It highlights the seismic social and cultural revolution that finally got London to swing. Suddenly it became the focus of the World for that, albeit brief moment in time ! Until then the word that best sums up Britain is "grey". Not quite sepia, but definitely monochrome.

That said, when I spend time in London now, I often fail to recognise the city that I grew up in and spent the first 30 years of my life in. I wonder if London is really my city anymore ? It is but at the same time it isn't . Maybe that is inevitable in any dynamic city that changes faster than we do as we age. It is beautifully assessed by Robert Elms in his terrific book *London Made Us - A Memoir of a Shape- Shifting City.*

Anyway, when we look back now from the cosiness of our iPhone, Facebook, dot com world, it is obvious that you have to get grief, anger, trauma out in the open as soon as you can. If you don't, it will appear sometime later and may eventually consume you. My ITP, I believe, was my response to stored up grief. I am convinced of it even though any specialist I have discussed it with is very sceptical. But they don't have any better explanation as to why I suddenly dropped into the purple zone.

I know that I must have the right (or is it wrong?) genetic make up to qualify me for ITP. Aside from that I don't have any explanation as to why the "other" conditions needed for me to trigger ITP, may have appeared. The only factor I can trace is delayed grief, trauma, shock. Sometimes ITP can be triggered by things like a virus, vaccination, certain drugs, but I had none of those events prior to my ITP break out in 2005/6.

So my theory is that in 2004 with the sudden death of my uncle, all the emotional issues that I had suppressed, following the death of my Dad in 1967, suddenly exploded. I think they literally sent my immune system into meltdown. Now for me, that excessive internal pressure finally erupted some time in 2004 and showed up with physical signs in early 2005. I remember having a few, shall we say, warning signs in 2004 and 2005 which I now firmly believe were ITP related. I could never have known it at the time.

On a holiday in Boston, Massachusetts in the Summer of 2004, I began to feel very dizzy, generally unwell. We had been having a tour of the Boston Red Sox stadium at Fenway Park and I just felt so ill. It had been a very hot day and I thought that perhaps I was just tired, possibly a bit dehydrated. Maybe it was the sight of the 'green monster". Even so we decided that I should get checked out at the Massachusetts General Hospital, just for peace of mind.

After checking my general condition, heart monitored for a few hours, blood and urine tests they couldn't find any issues and ended up just concluding that I may well have suffered a panic attack. I certainly had never had any panic attacks in my life before and I was sceptical that it was anything like that. Perhaps it was the curse of the Bambino. Nevertheless I was pleased to be advised there was nothing seriously wrong. But, at the time I had no idea that this turmoil in my body would later manifest itself as ITP. With hindsight this was a clear warning sign. Easy after the event though isn't it ?

The Boston incident was followed by another strange bout of wonkiness a year or so later on a ten day break in Las Vegas in October 2005. Again I felt so very tired and run down. We were staying at The Bellagio and I recall having breakfast one morning and feeling likel was going to pass out. At the time I just thought that it might be a combination of the stifling heat, jet lag and the after effects of our ten hour flight from London. But with hindsight it was probably another prelude to purple and a warning sign that my immune system was teetering on the edge of a precipice.

By Summer 2006, my emotional dam eventually burst, and the flood was unleashed in a purple river of an illness called ITP. What started out as The Thames ended up as The Nile ! Coupled with the stresses and strains of a very busy life and the inevitable pressures of work, my very own immune system tsunami struck with full force and was eventually diagnosed as ITP in the July (my least favourite month, for obvious reasons). Having read this book, you know the rest !

So there you have it, you have travelled along my ITP road and you now know why I think that I got onto that path in the first place. I cannot pretend that it has been anything but bumpy along the way but I know that I am better prepared for being purple than I was when I started out.

I truly hope that my journey has given some useful insights into the the mysteries of ITP and might help other sufferers know how to navigate their own individual purple journey better. As I mentioned early on in this book, there is no single ITP map. All any of us can do is draw on our own and each other's experiences to tailor our own bespoke guide.

My concluding thought is that no matter what ITP throws at you, it is imperative that you keep focused on living your life in the way that you want to. Make sure you are clear about the things that you really want to do and go do them ! Do them NOW ! As the late, great Ray Charles told the Boston Globe in 1983 - "Time is the most important component of life. You can't relive a moment. You can't redo it, patch it up. It's gone forever. I gotta go back to my Mom, she'd say, "Don't hope to do it. That's a waste of time. Just do it ". My biggest motivation is making the best use of the time I have in life ".

It is incredible to think that my purple time has gone by so quickly, almost thirteen years have rushed past in a flash. But it is worth remembering that time is actually, only a measure of events. It is vital that we all make those events memorable, special and filled with the things that we really really love.

So I believe that it is incumbent on all of us to create our very own purple patch and whatever that may be, wherever that is and with whomever we wish to share it, we then make sure that ITP does not get in the way.

You now have my full permission. As you've now read My Purple Patch, go ahead and find your very own one ! Don't let the purple, rain on your parade ! Always remember, that although we may be short of platelets on the odd occasion, the one commodity we are all definitely short of is time. We should all remember that and make the best use of it that we possibly can.

Platelets Up !

Acknowledgements

Many people often say that they might have a book in them. How often do you hear someone say that they 'could write a book", about their experiences, their life, their achievements ? Well I have never really been one of those people, at least, until ITP suddenly reared its' ugly head. I knew suddenly and completely by chance, that I had a story to tell.

Now that I have put my purple story down in words and recalled some pretty uncomfortable moments, I wanted to say a big THANK YOU to some of the people that have helped me during illness. If I have missed anyone, then I apologise in advance.

So a BIG THANK YOU to....

Shirley Watson MBE
Frank Watson
Dr Jecko Thachil
Professor James George
Dr Drew Provan
Dr Anh Ky To (Bob)
Mr Riffell
Mr K Penning

My ITP specialists since 2006 -

Dr G Morgenstern
Dr K Hassan
Dr Asif Khan
Dr K Ramasamy
Dr Pratap Neelakantan

All of the many nurses and phlebotomists at The Royal Berkshire Hospital who have held my hand through my ITP journey, especially everyone at West Ward.

My incredible Mum, my wonderful family and many friends who kept me on an even keel during the most turbulent of times. Thank you all for everything.

Almost last but by far from the least, my wonderful wife Amanda. Without her constant love and support I may not have completed this journey and certainly would not be half the person that I am.

Finally to my Dad, who through the impossibly short time we shared together, inspired me to be the person I have become and one I hope he would be proud of. Once, I was seven years old, now over half a century later, I am ITP positive and I miss him more than ever. Rest in Peace Dad, you'll forever be my inspiration.

About The Author

Anthony was born in 1960 in Charing Cross Hospital in The Strand, right in the heart of London. He was educated at St George the Martyr Primary School in Bloomsbury and Dame Alice Owens School Islington & Potters Bar. He studied banking and financial services at The London Metropolitan University in Moorgate. He became an Associate Member of the Chartered Institute of Bankers in 1987 and enjoyed al 30 year career in financial services. Anthony completed a Certificate in Humanities and a Batchelor of Arts degree with the Open University.

He was diagnosed with ITP in July 2006 and has worked as a volunteer for the ITP Support Association from 2010, where he set up and managed all of their social network platforms. He has written numerous articles about his ITP experiences for newspapers and magazines. He also wrote a regular column for the ITP Support Association publication The Platelet, and continues to make regular written contributions.

He actively promotes ITP awareness through his blog and social media platforms. He has made a number of ITP presentations to varied audiences from pharmaceutical companies to healthcare professionals. He takes an active part in the annual Rare Disease Day awareness campaign organised by Rare Disease UK.

When not writing or talking about his ITP, he spends far too much time and energy supporting Tottenham Hotspur Football Club, the England Cricket and Rugby Union teams and following any sport far too keenly for his wife's good. He is an avid reader and takes a keen interest in current affairs, history, politics and economics. He is an eternal optimist and is naturally progressive.

His other passions are music, clothes, film, gardening, food, photography, art, architecture, social history, London, researching family history, travel and writing about the things that really matter to him. The rest of his time he just squanders !

He can be found at the following locations....

TWITTER ..... @AnthonyH7 and @Patch1Purple

INSTAGRAM https://www.instagram.com/anthonyheard1960/

My Purple Patch - ITP Blog ..... http://anthonyheard.simplesite.com

TUMBLR - Something to Write Home About Blog ..... https://www.tumblr.com/blog/ anthonypaulh

Appendix

BIBLIOGRAPHY - Other Books and sources which may tickle your platelets

BLOG-*Katie Cleary Autoimmune Mom*…http://www.autoimmunemom.com/about

BLOG - *Frances Ryan- Just Frances* - http://justfrances.com/archive

WEB SITE - *ITP and Me* - http://itpandme.com/your-stories

WEB SITE - *The Steven Sims Cavaliers Foundation* - www.cavaliers.foundation

BOOK - *Heartaches and Miracles : My Struggles with Immune Thrombocytopenic Purpura* - by Greta Burroughs .

BOOK - *Wish by Spiri*t : *A Journey of Recovery & Healing From an Autoimmune Blood Disease* - By Joan W Young .

BOOK - *How to Heal a Bruise : For Patients and Families Living with Immune Thrombocytopenia* - By Meghan Brewster .

BOOK - *Bellies, Babies and Bruises : An ITP Book for Women and Babies* - By Meghan Brewster.

BOOK - *When The Body Says No - The Cost of Hidden Stress* - By Dr Gabor Mate.

BOOK - *Going on the Turn : Being the Extraordinary Stories of my Life and Dodging Death's Door* - By Danny Baker

BOOK - *Ready Steady Go : Swinging London and the Invention of Cool* - by Shawn Levy

BOOK - *London Made Us : A Memoir of a Shape-Shifting City* - by Robert Elms